Modern French Dictionary

French-English and English-French

kasahorow

We are all Africans

Revised 2020-03-24

© 2012

KWID: A-10000-FR-EN-2020-03-24

Esi S.

Matières

Preface

kasahorow aime French

Our mission is to give African languages speakers in the world freedom by modernizing African languages.

The first step to modern French usage is to write French with consistent spelling rules. Consistent spelling may be pronounced in different ways in different places.

In other words, the spelling of a word does not indicate how to pronounce it. In fact, there is no correct pronunciation. Rather, we think your pronunciation is correct when you can be understood by others.

Sign up to receive updates in your favourite African language at kasahorow.org.

Sharing License

You may freely photocopy and redistribute this book for private or commercial use. No restrictions. Yes go ahead. Do good by sharing.

Errata

All mistakes are ours. When you find one, please let us know so we can fix it.

Please send corrections and feedback to help@kasahorow.org or online at kasahorow.org/booktalk.

Read This Dictionary

There are different types of words in each language. Each type of word has a function in a sentence.

Here are some word types used in this dictionary:

Type	Meaning
nom	*nom* - a noun is a name
adj	An *adjective* shows the quality of a noun
pro	A *pronoun* points to a noun

act	A *verb* is an action
adv	An *adverb* shows the intensity of a verb
det	A *determiner* article
pos	A *possessive* pronoun

If you are reading and you never have to use a dictionary, then it means you are ready to read more advanced texts! Well done!

We wish you many happy reading adventures in French and English

kasahorow Editors & Translators
help@kasahorow.org

PS: This dictionary is also available online (with even more words) at
fr.kasahorow.org/app/d

Français-English

œ à a â b c ç d e é ê f g h i î j k l m n o p q r s t u v w x y z

œuf^{nom.masculin} egg
poulet œuf chicken egg
à^{pre} to
de ici à là from here to there
à^{pre} at
rencontrez moi meet me
à l'étranger^{nom} abroad
ma à l'étranger my abroad
à l'extérieur^{nom} outdoors
allez à l'extérieur go outdoors
à l'intérieur^{adv} inside
allez inside go inside
à l'intérieur^{pre} inside
à l'intérieur la pot inside the pot
abdomen^{nom} abdomen
sa abdomen her abdomen
abeille^{nom} bee
un abeille fait miel a bee makes honey
abomination^{nom.feminin} abomination
il est une abomination it is an abomination
aborigène^{nom.masculin} aborigine
il est un aborigène he is an aborigine
aboyer^{act} bark
un chien aboye a dog barks
abricot^{nom.masculin} apricot
ton abricot your apricot
accentuation^{exc} emphasis
je êtes I are
acceptation^{nom} acceptance
amour, acceptation et pardon love, acceptance and forgiveness
accepter^{act} accept
nous acceptons le cadeau we accept the gift
accès^{nom} access
ta accès your access
accident^{nom} accident
voiture accident car accident
accouchement^{nom} childbirth
un accouchement apporte joie a childbirth brings joy
accuser^{act} accuse
je accuse I accuse
acheter^{act} buy
elles acheteront un voiture they will buy a car
acheteur^{nom} buyer
ma acheteur my buyer
achever^{act} fulfil
ell'acheve le travail she fulfils the work

acide^{adj} acidic
eau acide acidic water
acide^{nom.masculin} acid
"HCl" est un acide "HCl" is an acid
acte^{nom} act
acte act
acteur^{nom.masculin} actor
il est un acteur he is an actor
action^{nom} action
ma action my action
activité^{nom} activity
sa activité her activity
actrice^{nom.feminin} actress
ell'est une actrice she is an actress
addition^{nom} addition
sa addition her addition
adjectif^{nom.masculin} adjective
le nom a un adjectif the noun has an adjective
administration^{nom} administration
sa administration apporte progrès her administration brings advancement
admirer^{act} admire
tu admires you admire
adopter^{act} adopt
ell'adopte she adopts
adoption^{nom} adoption
ma adoption my adoption
adorer^{act} worship
je adore I worship
adoucir^{act} soften
adoucissez ta voix soften your voice
adresse^{nom} address
ta adresse your address
adulation^{nom} adulation
elle mérite adulation she deserves adulation
adultère^{nom} adultery
adultère et divorce adultery and divorce
adverbe^{nom.masculin} adverb
le verbe a un adverbe the verb has an adverb
aeroport^{nom.masculin} airport
son aeroport her airport
affaires^{nom} business
ma affaires my business
affamé^{adj} hungry
il est affamé it is hungry
affecter^{nom.masculin} affect
son affecter her affect

affiler^{act} sharpen
affilez un couteau sharpen a knife
Africain^{nom} African
ta Africain your African
Afrikaans^{nom.masculin} Afrikaans
ell'écri Afrikaans she records Afrikaans
Afrique^{nom} Africa
ta Afrique your Africa
âge^{nom} age
ta âge your age
agneau^{nom} lamb
agneau de dieu lamb of god
agréable^{adj} pleasant
un personne agréable a pleasant person
agréable^{adj.masculin} nice
il est agréable he is nice
agression^{nom} aggression
sa agression her aggression
agriculteur^{nom} farmer
ell'est un agriculteur she is a farmer
ah^{exc} ah
ah yes! ah yes!
aider^{act} help
tu aides you help
aiguille^{nom} needle
chaîne et aiguille string and needle
aile^{nom} wing
un oiseau a ailes deux a bird has two wings
aimer^{act} love
j'aime ma femme I love my wife
aimer^{act} like
I like eating
aîné^{adj} elder
ma enfant de mêmes parents aîné my elder sibling
aine^{nom} groin
aine de un homme groin of a man
ainsi^{cjn} so
why so? why so?
air^{nom} air
l'air est the air is
aisselle^{nom} armpit
sa aisselle her armpit
ajouter^{act} add
ajoutez sucre add sugar
ajuster^{act} adjust
ell'ajuste she adjusts

Akan^{nom} Akan
Akan est un langue Akan is a language
alcool^{nom.masculin} alcohol
il boi alcool he drinks alcohol
alerter^{act} alert
alertez them alert them
Algérie^{nom} Algeria
ma Algérie my Algeria
alléluia^{exc} hallelujah
chantez hallelujah sing hallelujah
aller^{act} go
nous allons we go
alliance^{nom} covenant
ma alliance my covenant
poivre d'alligator^{nom} alligator pepper
sa poivre d'alligator her alligator pepper
allumer^{act} kindle
allumez un feu kindle a fire
allumer^{act} switch on
tu allumes you switch on
âme^{nom} soul
ma âme exulte my soul exults
amen^{exc} amen
alléluia et amen hallelujah and amen
amer^{adj} bitter
la médecine est amer the drug is bitter
Américain^{nom.masculin} American
son Américain her American
Américaine female American

Amérique^{nom.masculin} America
mon Amérique my America
Amharique^{nom.masculin} Amharic
son Amharique her Amharic
ami^{nom} friend
ma ami a un maison my friend has a house
amour^{nom} love
paix et amour peace and love
amusant^{adj} funny
l'histoire est amusant the story is funny
amusant^{adj.masculin} amusing
il est amusant it is amusing
ancêtre^{nom} ancestor
ma ancêtre my ancestor
ancien^{adj.masculin} ancient
maison ancien ancient house
ancre^{nom} anchor
ancre de un navire anchor of a ship

âne^{nom} donkey

ma âne my donkey

Anglais^{nom} English

nous lisons Anglais we read English

angle^{nom} angle

sa angle her angle

Angleterre^{nom.masculin} England

ton Angleterre your England

anguille^{nom} eel

sa anguille her eel

animal^{nom} animal

un chien est un animal a dog is an animal

animal de compagnie^{nom.masculin} pet

mon animal de compagnie my pet

année^{nom} year

un année nouveau a a new year has

annonce^{nom} announcement

lisez l'annonce read the announcement

annoncer^{act} announce

annoncer announce

annuel^{adj} yearly

il est annuel it is yearly

annuler^{act} annul

annulez un mariage annul a marriage

annuler^{act} cancel

annulez la réunion cancel the meeting

antilope^{nom.masculin} antelope

un lion aime antilope viande a lion likes antelope meat

antiquité^{nom} antiquity

ta antiquité your antiquity

Août^{nom} August

Août est un mois August is a month

apathie^{nom} apathy

apathie tuez bon apathy kill good

Apodidae^{nom.masculin} swift

l'oiseau est un Apodidae the bird is a swift

appareil photographique^{nom} camera

lentille de un appareil photographique lens of a camera

apparition^{nom} apparition

ta apparition your apparition

appeler^{act} call

appeler le garçon to call the boy

appellation^{nom} appellation

sa appellation her appellation

applaudir^{act} clap

tu applaudis you clap

apporter^{act} bring

il apportera un livre he will bring a book

apprendre^{act} learn

ell'apprend she learns

approcher^{act} approach

je approche I approach

appuyer^{act} press

tu appuyes you press

après-midi^{nom} afternoon

l'après-midi est chaud the afternoon is hot

arachide^{nom} groundnut

maïs et arachide corn and groundnut

araignée^{nom} spider

sa araignée her spider

arc^{nom.masculin} bow

arc et flèche bow and arrow

arc-en-ciel^{nom} rainbow

je voyez un arc-en-ciel I see a rainbow

ardoise^{nom} slate

essuyez l'ardoise wipe the slate

argent^{nom} money

l'argent aidera the money will help

argent^{nom} silver

argent et or silver and gold

argent^{nom.masculin} cash

je avez argent I have cash

argile^{nom} clay

argile vase clay vase

argument^{nom} argument

ma argument my argument

arme^{nom} weapon

ta arme your weapon

arrêter^{act} cease

arrêter la bruit cease the noise

arrière^{nom} back

l'arrière de la porte the back of the door

arrière petit-enfant^{nom.masculin} great-grandchild

son arrière petit-enfant his great-grandchild

arrière-garde^{nom} rearguard

ma arrière-garde my rearguard

arriver^{act} arrive

ell'arrive she arrives

arrogance^{nom.masculin} arrogance

arrogance est mauvais arrogance is bad

arrogant^{adj.masculin} arrogant

homme arrogant arrogant man

artère^{nom} artery

un artère grand a large artery

articulation^{nom} joint
 ma articulation my joint
artiste^{nom.masculin} artist
 ell'est un artiste she is an artist
Asie^{nom.masculin} Asia
 mon Asie my Asia
aspiration^{nom.masculin} aspiration
 aspiration bon good aspiration
assiette^{nom} dish
 lavez ta assiette launder your dish
assistance^{nom.masculin} assistance
 il a besoin de ton assistance he needs your assistance
assistant^{nom} assistant
 ma assistant my assistant
association^{nom} association
 ta association your association
asticot^{nom} maggot
 ma asticot my maggot
atelier^{nom.masculin} workshop
 nous avons un atelier we have a workshop
atlantique^{adj.masculin} Atlantic
 Océan Atlantique Atlantic Ocean
attacher^{act} attach
 attachez à mur attach to wall
attacher^{act} tie
 nous attachons we tie
atteindre^{act} reach
 demain, il atteindra la maison tomorrow, he will reach the house
attendre^{act} wait
 nous attendsons we wait
atterrir^{act} land
 tu atterris you land
attraper^{act} catch
 je attrape le balle I catch the ball
au loin^{nom.masculin} Afar
 il écri au loin he records Afar
au revoir^{exc} fare well
 au revoir, ma ami fare well, my friend
aube^{nom} daybreak
 aube et tombée de la nuit daybreak and nightfall

aube^{nom} dawn
 un aube nouveau a new dawn
auditeur^{nom} listener
 ma auditeur my listener

augmenter^{act} arise
 nous augmentons we arise
augmenter^{act} raise
 augmentez ta main raise your hand
augmenter^{act} increase
 tu augmentes you increase
aujourd'hui^{adv} today
 ell'arrive aujourd'hui she arrives today
aussi^{adv} too
 aussi lentement too slowly
Australie^{nom.masculin} Australia
 nous aimons Australie we love Australia
automne^{nom.masculin} Autumn
 ton automne your Autumn
autoroute^{nom} highway
 ta autoroute your highway
autre^{adj.masculin} other
 un temps autre an other time
aux jambes arquées^{adj} bow-legged
 homme aux jambes arquées bow-legged man
avaler^{act} swallow
 ell'avale she swallows
avance^{adj} advance
 il est avance it is advance
avant^{pre} before
 mangez eat
avant^{nom} front
 l'avant du livre the front of the book
avantage^{nom} advantage
 ta avantage your advantage
avare^{nom} miser
 il est un avare he is a miser
avare^{adj} miserly
 il est avare he is miserly
avarice^{nom} stinginess
 sa avarice her stinginess
avenir^{nom} future
 mu avenir my future
avertir^{act} warn
 avertissez someone warn someone
avertissement^{nom} warning
 écoutez à l'avertissement listen to the warning
avidité^{nom.feminin} greed
 avidité et envie gred and envy
avion^{nom} aeroplane
 sa avion her aeroplane
avocat^{nom} lawyer
 sa avocat her lawyer

avoirct have
ell'a argent she has money
avoir besoin dect need
j'ai besoin de I need
ayantro having
thé de sucre tea of sugar
azontoom azonto
ma azonto my azonto
bœufom beef
nous mangeons bœuf we eat beef
babouinom baboon
ta babouin your baboon
baignerct bathe
je baigne jour chaque I bathe every day
bâillerct yawn
nous bâillons we yawn
bainom.masculin bath
nettoyer le bain clean the bath
baiserct kiss
baisez kiss
balaiom broom
balai et balayette broom and dustpan
balançoireom swing
jouez un balançoire play a swing
balayerct sweep
elle balaye la sol she sweeps the floor
balayetteom.masculin dustpan
balai et balayette broom and dustpan
baleineom whale
un baleine grand a large whale
balleom.masculin ball
jeu balle play ball
balleom.masculin bullet
ma balle my bullet
ballonom balloon
sa ballon her balloon
Bambaraom.masculin Bambara
Bambara langue Bambara language
bambinom toddler
bambin, où toddler, where
bananeom banana
le singe aime la banane the monkey likes the banana
bancom bench
un banc blanc a white bench
banqueom bank
ma argent est à la banque my money is at the bank

baouléom.nouveau.masculin Baule
je apprendras baoulé I will learn Baule
baptêmeom baptism
repentance et baptême repentance and baptism
baptiserct baptise
baptisez John baptise John
barbeom beard
barbe longue long beard
barilom barrel
ma baril my barrel
basilicom.masculin basil
un basilic feuille a basil leaf
basketballom.masculin basketball
elle joue basketball she plays basketball
bassinom basin
ma bassin my basin
batailleom battle
sa bataille her battle
bateauom.masculin boat
bateau rouge red boat
bâtimentom.masculin building
le bâtiment est nouveau the building is new
bâtonom stick
cassez la bâton break the stick
batteurom drummer
ell'est un batteur she is a drummer
battrect beat
battsez someone beat someone
baume à lèvresom.masculin lipbalm
ton baume à lèvres your lipbalm
beau-enfantom.masculin step-child
mon beau-enfant my step-child
beau-pèreom.masculin stepfather
mon beau-père aime la nourriture my stepfather likes the food
beaucoupdj plenty
il est beaucoup it is plenty
beaucoupdj.masculin many
nous avons beaucoup we have many
beautéom beauty
beauté et amour beauty and love
bébéom baby
j'ai un bébé I have a baby
belledj beautiful
tu es belle you are beautiful
bénédictionom blessing
la bénédiction de Dieu the blessing of God

Bénin^{nom} Benin
ma Bénin my Benin
bénir^{act} bless
bénissez me bless me
beurre^{nom} butter
pain et beurre bread and butter
beurre de karité^{nom} sheabutter
la parfum de beurre de karité the fragrance of sheabutter
bible^{nom} bible
la bibl'et la Coran the bible and the koran
bibliothèque^{nom} library
sa bibliothèque her library
bien^{adv} well
faites il do it
bien^{nom} good
ta bien your good
bien^{adj} well
il est bien it is well
bien fait^{exc} well done
bien fait Sah well done Sah
bien que^{cjn} though

bien-aimé^{nom} darling
ma bien-aimé a my darling has
bien-aimé^{nom.masculin} beloved
ton bien-aimé your beloved
bientôt^{adv} soon
ell'est she is
bienvenue^{exc} welcome
bienvenue, bienvenue welcome, welcome
bière^{nom} beer
nous boisons bière we drink beer
bile^{nom} bile
bile vert green bile
billet^{nom} ticket
regardez à ma billet look at my ticket
biologie^{nom} biology
sa biologie her biology
blague^{nom} joke
sa blague her joke
blanc^{adj} white
maison blanc white house
blé^{nom} wheat
ma blé my wheat
blesser^{act} injure
nous blessons we injure

bleu^{adj} blue
la robe est bleu the dress is blue
Blog^{nom} blog
nourriture Blog food blog
bloquer^{act} block
tu bloques you block
boire^{act} drink
tu bois you drink
bois de chauffage^{nom} firewood
pickup bois de chauffage pickup firewood
boîte^{nom} box
un boîte grand a big box
bol^{nom.masculin} bowl
un bol rouge a red bowl
bombe^{nom} bomb
la bombe explosez the bomb explode
bon^{adj} good
Dieu fait bon God does good
bon anniversaire^{exc} happy birthday
bon anniversaire Doris happy birthday Doris
bon après-midi^{exc} good afternoon
après-midi bon good afternoon
bon travail^{exc} good job

bonheur^{nom} happiness
bonheur a happiness has
bonjour^{exc} good morning
matin bon good morning
bonne année^{exc} happy new year
bonne année happy new year
bonne soirée^{exc} good evening
soir bon good evening
bonté^{nom} goodness
bonté et miséricorde goodness and mercy
bonus^{nom.masculin} bonus
je voulois un bonus I want a bonus
bosquet^{nom} grove
sa bosquet her grove
bouche^{nom} mouth
ma bouche my mouth
boucle d'oreille^{nom.feminin} earring
il porte boucle d'oreille he wears earring
bouclier^{nom} shield
il est ma bouclier he is my shield
boue^{nom} mud
lavez la boue launder the mud
bouffon^{nom} jester
ell'est un bouffon she is a jester

bouillie[nom] porridge
mil bouillie millet porridge
bouillie[nom] pap
mangez la bouillie eat the pap
bouillir[act] boil
il bouillit he boils
boulot[nom.masculin] job
je avez besoin de un boulot I need a job
bourgeon[nom] bud
fleur bourgeon flower bud
bourreau[nom] executioner
ma bourreau my executioner
bourse[nom] scholarship
je avez un bourse I have a scholarship
bouse[nom] dung
vache bouse cow dung
bouteille[nom] bottle
ma bouteille my bottle
boutique[nom.feminin] shop
ma boutique my shop
bouton[nom] pimple
je avez un bouton I have a pimple
bouton[nom.masculin] button
appuyer le bouton press the button
boxe[nom.feminin] boxing
boxe est un sport boxing is a sport
branche[nom] branch
famille branche family branch
brancher[act] branch
elle branche she branchs
bras[nom] arm
ta bras your arm
bref[adj] brief
il est bref it is brief
brillant[adj] bright
la chambre est brillant the room is bright
briller[act] shine
elle brille she shines
brique[nom] brick
ta brique your brick
brosse[nom] brush
un brosse noir a black brush
brosse à dents[nom] toothbrush
brosse à dents et dentifrice toothbrush and tooth-paste
brousse[nom] bush

bruit[nom] noise
ta bruit your noise
brûler[act] burn
brûlez papers burn papers
brûlures d'estomac[nom] heartburn
je avez brûlures d'estomac I have heartburn
brume[nom] mist
matin brume morning mist
brun[adj] brown
l'oiseau est brun the bird is brown
brute[nom] bully
il est un brute he is a bully
budget[nom] budget
sa budget her budget
bungalow[nom.masculin] bungalow
mon bungalow my bungalow
bureau[nom] office
la bureau de ma mère the office of my mother
bureau de poste[nom] post office
sa bureau de poste her post office
Burkina Faso[nom] Burkina Faso
ma Burkina Faso my Burkina Faso
bus[nom.masculin] bus
le bus est rouge the bus is red
but[nom.masculin] aim
le but de vie the aim of life
cœur[nom] heart
cœur bon good heart
ça[pro] it

cacao[nom] cocoa
cacao arbre cocoa tree
cacher[act] hide
cacher derrière la porte to hide behind the door
cadavre[nom] corpse
la cadavre est the corpse is
cadeau[nom.masculin] gift
cadeau bon good gift
cadre[nom] framework
la cadre de la maison the framework of the house
cafard[nom] cockroach
je voyez un cafard I see a cockroach
café[nom.masculin] coffee
elle boisez café she drink coffee
calendrier[nom.masculin] calendar
un calendrier nouveau a new calendar
Californie[nom] California
l'état de Californie the state of California

calme^{adj} quiet
elles sont calme they are quiet
cambriolage^{nom} burglary
cambriolage est burglary is
caméléon^{nom} chameleon
je voyez la caméléon I see the chameleon
Cameroun^{nom} Cameroon
ta Cameroun your Cameroon
camp^{nom} camp
allez à la camp go to the camp
Canada^{nom.masculin} Canada
ton Canada your Canada
canapé^{nom.masculin} sofa
mon canapé my sofa
canard^{nom.masculin} duck
canard blanc white duck
cancer^{nom} cancer
cancer est un maladie cancer is a disease
caniveau^{nom} gutter
ta caniveau your gutter
canne^{nom.feminin} cane
apportez la canne bring the cane
canne à sucre^{nom} sugarcane
ta canne à sucre your sugarcane
canon^{nom} cannon
tirez la canon shoot the cannon
capable^{adj} capable
un femme capable a capable woman
capitaine^{nom} captain
ell'est un capitaine she is a captain
capitale^{nom} capital
la capitale de Ghana the capital of Ghana
caractère^{nom} character
sa caractère her character
Caraïbes^{nom.pluriel} Caribbean
sa Caraïbes her Caribbean
caramel^{nom} toffee
léchez un caramel lick a toffee
caresser^{act} caress
sa main caressez il her hand caress it
carotte^{nom.feminin} carrot
ma carotte my carrot
carte^{nom} map
lisez la carte read the map
carte^{nom} card
un carte blanc a white card
carton^{nom.masculin} carton
carton de lait carton of milk

casser^{act} break
cassez la bâton break the stick
casserole^{nom} pan
casserole vieux old pan
casserole^{nom} saucepan
cuisez dans la casserole cook in the saucepan
cast^{nom.masculin} cast
cast de un film cast of a film
catarrhe^{nom} catarrh
je avez catarrhe I have catarrh
catégorie^{nom} category
ta catégorie your category
ce^{det} that
ce chien that dog
ce^{det.feminin.masculin} this
prêtez moi lend me
cedi^{nom} cedi
pesewa cent faites cedi un hundred pesewa make
one cedi
ceinture^{nom.feminin} belt
ceinture noir black belt
cellule^{nom.feminin} cell
la peau a cellules the skin has cells
cendre^{nom} ash
sel et cendre salt and ash
cent^{adj} hundred
cent hundred
cependant^{cjn} however

cercle^{nom} circle
cercl'et ligne circle and line
cerf^{nom} deer
un lion aime cerfs a lion likes deers
certains^{pro} some
certains veniront some will come
certificat^{nom} certificate
ta certificat your certificate
cerveau^{nom} brain
la cerveau et l'esprit the brain and the mind
ces^{pro} these
elles voient ces they see these
ces^{det} these
ces books these books
cet^{pro} this
cet est le tiens this is yours
cette^{pro} that
cette est le tiens that is yours

cette chose that thing

cette personne that person

chacunpro each and everyone
nous aimons chacun we love each and everyone
chagrineract grieve
ma âme chagrine my soul grieves
chaînenom string
chaîne et aiguille string and needle
chaînenom chain
ma chaîne my chain
chairnom flesh
chair et sang flesh and blood
chaisenom chair
elles apportent la chaise they bring the chair
châlitnom.masculin bedstead
mon châlit my bedstead
chambrenom room
sa chambre her room
chambrenom bedroom
ta chambre your bedroom
chameaunom camel
ta chameau est vieux your camel is old
champignonnom mushroom
champignon soupe mushroom soup
chanceuxadj.masculin lucky
fille chanceux lucky girl
changenom.feminin change
ta change your change
changeract adapt
temps change tout time adapts everything
chansonnom song
jouer un chanson play a song
chanteract sing
nous chantons we sing
chaotiqueadj chaotic
la place est chaotique the place is chaotic
chapeaunom hat
ma chapeau my hat
chapitrenom chapter
chapitre chapter
chaqueadj each
chose chaque each thing
chaqueadj.masculin every
maison chaque every house
charbon de boisnom charcoal
sac de charbon de bois sack of charcoal

chargesci charge
un électron a charge an electron has charge
charpentiernom carpenter
il a besoin de un charpentier he needs a carpenter

chasseract chase
le chien chasse the dog chases
chatnom.masculin cat
le chat a un queue the cat has a tail
chaudadj hot
l'eau est chaud the water is hot
chaussettenom sock
sa chaussette her sock
chaussurenom shoe
ta chaussure your shoe
chauve sourisnom.feminin bat
ma chauve souris my bat
chefnom chief
ell'est un chef she is a chief
chefnom chef
un chef bon a good chef
chefnom.masculin leader
ton chef your leader
chef de clannom.masculin chieftain
mon chef de clan my chieftain
cheminnom path
suitez la chemin follow the path
chemisenom.feminin shirt
ma chemise my shirt
chenillenom caterpillar
un chenille devenit un papillon a caterpillar becomes a butterfly
chèquenom.masculin cheque
écrisez un chèque record a cheque
cheradj expensive
il est cher it is expensive
chevalnom.masculin horse
cheval blanc white horse
cheveuxnom.pluriel hair
poitrine cheveux chest hair
chevillenom ankle
sa cheville her ankle
chèvrenom.feminin goat
une chèvre et un a goat and a
Chewanom Chewa
sa Chewa her Chewa
chiennom.masculin dog
un chien aboye a dog barks

chiffon^{nom} cloth
portez chiffon wear cloth
chimie^{nom} chemistry
nous apprendsons chimie we learn chemistry
chimpanzé^{nom} chimpanzee
je voyez un chimpanzé I see a chimpanzee
chocolat^{nom.masculin} chocolate
le chocolat a the chocolate has
choisir^{act} choose
choisir bien choose good
chose^{nom} thing
chose un one thing
chrétien^{nom} Christian
ta chrétien your Christian
Christ^{nom.masculin} Christ
mon Christ my Christ
Christianisme^{nom} Christianity
sa Christianisme her Christianity
cicatrice^{nom} scar
sa joue a un cicatrice her cheek has a scar
ciel^{nom} sky
la ciel et le soleil the sky and the sun
cigarette^{nom} cigarette
ma cigarette my cigarette
cil^{nom} eyelash
cil noir black eyelash
ciment^{nom} cement
sa ciment her cement
cinéma^{nom} cinema
nous aimons la cinéma we like the cinema
cinq^{adj} five
cinq five
cinq personnes^{nom} five persons
ma cinq personnes my five persons
cinquante^{adj} fifty
cinquante fifty
circonstance^{nom} circumstance
sa circonstance her circumstance
circulation^{nom} traffic
circulation lumière traffic light
ciseaux^{nom} scissors
ma ciseaux my scissors
citoyen^{nom} citizen
je suis un citoyen de terre I am a citizen of earth
citron^{nom.masculin} lemon
citrons troiss three lemons
citron vert^{nom} lime
citron vert juice lime juice

civilisé^{adj} civilized
un monde civilisé a civilized world
clair^{adj.masculin} clear
ciel clair clear sky
clairement^{adv} clearly
tu voyez il you see it
clairon^{adj.masculin} clarion
un avertissement clairon a clarion warning
clavier^{nom} keyboard
appuyer "k" sur la clavier press "k" on the keyboard
clé^{nom} key
ta clé your key
clémence^{nom} leniency
ta clémence your leniency
client^{nom.masculin} customer
un client bon a good customer
cliquer^{act} click
cliquez ici click here
cloche^{nom} bell
école cloche school bell
clôture^{nom} fence
ma clôture my fence
clou de girofle^{nom.masculin} clove
ajoutez un clou de girofle add a clove
coaltar^{nom} coaltar
coaltar chaud hot coaltar
cobra^{nom} cobra
cobra noir black cobra
code^{nom} code
ta code your code
coiffures^{nom} headgear
ta coiffures your headgear
coins^{nom} corners
ta coins your corners
coller^{act} paste
nous collons we paste
collier^{nom} necklace
ivoire collier ivory necklace
colline^{nom} hill
colline top hill top
colombe^{nom} dove
colombe blanc white dove
colonne vertébrale^{nom} spine
oreille, nez et colonne vertébrale ear, nose and spine
colorant^{nom} dye
colorant noir black dye

colorieract colour
colorier et apprendre colour and learn
combienadj how much
il est combien it is how much
comfortableadj.masculin comfortable
le canapé est comfortable the sofa is comfortable
comiténom.masculin committee
je se raccorder le comité I will join the committee

commandenom command
sa commande her command
commanderact command
tu commandes you command
commeadv as

commeadv like
il sentit comme fufu it feels like fufu
commepre like

comme celle-ciexc such as this
un personne a person
commenceract begin
tu commences you begin
commenceract start
nous commencons we start
commentadv how
comment how
comment allez-vousexc how do you are
bonjour et comment allez-vous how do you do are
hello and
commerçantnom trader
je suis un commerçant I am a trader
commercenom trade
un commerce bon a good trade
communauténom community
un communauté de gens a community of people
compétencenom skill
ta compétence your skill
comportementnom behaviour
comportement normal normal behaviour
compréhensionnom.feminin comprehension
compréhension est important comprehension is
important
comprendreact understand
tu comprends you understand
comptenom account
banque compte bank account

compteract count
nous comptons l'argent we count the money
comptesnom accounts
sa comptes her accounts
conducteurnom driver
la conducteur a the driver has
conduireact lead
conduisez us lead us
conduireact drive
conduisez un voiture drive a car
conférencenom conference
ta conférence your conference
confiancenom.feminin trust
ma confiance my trust
confiancenom confidence
je avez confiance I have confidence
confortnom comfort
ta confort your comfort
Congonom Congo
ma Congo my Congo
conjonctionnom.feminin conjunction

conjonctivitenom.feminin conjunctivitis
conjonctivite est un maladie conjunctivitis is a disease
connaissancenom knowledge
connaissance et sagesse knowledge and wisdom
connaîtreact know
je connaîtsez I know
connexionnom.feminin connection
ce chaîne a un connexion this chain has one connection
consciencenom conscience
ta conscience your conscience
conseillernom councillor
ell'est un conseiller she is a councillor
conseilsnom advice
un prêtre a conseils a pastor has advice
conséquencenom consequence
ta conséquence your consequence
conservateurnom preservative
sa conservateur her preservative
consolationnom consolation
amour et consolation love and consolation
constitueract consist
je constitue I consist
construireact build
nous construisons un maison we build a house

continent^{nom} continent
African continent African continent
continuer^{act} continue
continuez le travail continue the work
cool^{adj} cool
un bière cool a cool beer
copain$^{nom.masculin}$ boyfriend
mon copain my boyfriend
copieux$^{adj.masculin}$ plentiful
la nourriture est copieux the food is plentiful
coquelet$^{nom.masculin}$ cockerel
un coquelet est a cockerel is
coquille^{nom} shell
coquille de un crabe shell of a crab
Coran^{nom} koran
la bibl'et la Coran the bible and the koran
corbeau^{nom} crow
un corbeau noir a black crow
corde^{nom} rope
un corde longue a long rope
coriandre$^{nom.feminin}$ cilantro
coriandre est un plante cilantro is a plant
corne^{nom} horn
corne musique horn music
corne de guerre^{nom} warhorn
ma corne de guerre my warhorn
corps$^{nom.masculin}$ body
son corps her body
corsage^{nom} bodice
elle porte un corsage she wears a bodice
costume^{nom} suit
elle porte un costume she wears a suit
côte^{nom} coast
or côte gold coast
Côte d'Ivoire^{nom} Cote d'Ivoire
sa Côte d'Ivoire her Cote d'Ivoire
coton^{nom} cotton
coton est blanc cotton is white
cou$^{nom.masculin}$ neck
la cravate pend son cou the tie hangs his neck
coucher du soleil^{nom} sunset

coudre^{act} sew
coudsez chiffon sew cloth
couler^{act} sink
nous coulons we sink
couler^{act} flow
l'eau coule the water flows

couleur^{nom} color
j'aime ta couleur I like your color
coup^{nom} blow
ta coup your blow
couper^{act} cut
couper la journal cut the paper
cour^{nom} yard
cour grand big yard
courage^{nom} courage
ell'a courage she has courage
courageux^{adj} brave
homme courageux brave man
courageux$^{adj.masculin}$ courageous
il est courageux it is courageous
coureur de jupons^{nom} philanderer
sa coureur de jupons her philanderer
courir^{act} run
nous courissons we run
couronne^{nom} crown
un couronne de or a crown of gold
course^{nom} race
courissez un course run a race
petit^{adj} short
ce homme est petit this man is short
cousin$^{nom.masculin}$ cousin
mon cousin my cousin
coût^{nom} cost
ta coût your cost
couteau$^{nom.masculin}$ knife
affilez un couteau sharpen a knife
coutelas^{nom} cutlass
ma coutelas my cutlass
coutume^{nom} custom
amour est un coutume bon love is a good custom
couvercle^{nom} lid
couvercle de un tasse lid of a cup
couverture^{nom} blanket
couverture mouillé wet blanket
couvrir^{act} cover
couvrissez il cover it
covetuousness^{nom} covetuousness
sa covetuousness her covetuousness
crabe^{nom} crab
crabe aime eau crab likes water
craie$^{nom.masculin}$ chalk
craie blanc white chalk
crâne^{nom} skull
ma crâne my skull

crasseuxadj.masculin filthy
la maison est crasseux the house is filthy
cravatenom tie
la cravate pend son cou the tie hangs his neck
crayonnom.masculin pencil
prendre le crayon take the pencil
créateurnom.masculin creator
créateur dieu creator god
créationnom creation
tout création all creation
créeract create
quelque chose créez nouveau something create new

creuseract dig
elle creuse she digs
crevettenom shrimp
ma crevette my shrimp
crieract shout
je crie I shout
crieract yell
tu cries you yell
cristalnom criestal
un cristal belle a beautiful criestal
crocodilenom crocodile
un crocodil'aime eau a crocodile likes water
croireact believe
elle croi l'enfant she believes the child
croissancenom.feminin growth
croissance est bon growth is good
croixnom cross
la croix de Christ the cross of Christ
croupenom rump
regardez à sa croupe look at his rump
cubenom cube
un cube de sucre a cube of sugar
cuillèrenom spoon
sa cuillère her spoon
cuireact bake
cuisez pain bake bread
cuireact cook
cuire la nourriture to cook the food
cuisinenom kitchen
sa cuisine her kitchen
cuissenom thigh
poulet cuisse chicken thigh
culturenom culture
la culture de mon école the culture of my school

cymbalenom cymbal
jouez la cymbale play the cymbal
damenom lady
dame Danso lady Danso
dangernom danger
il est dans danger he is in danger
dangereuxadj dangerous
un jeu dangereux a dangerous game
danspre in
regarder dans la pot look in the pot
danseract dance
danser bien to dance well
datenom date
je connaîts la date I know the date
depre of
langue de Afrique language of Africa
depre about
de toi about you
depre from
allez go
de bonne heureadj early
matin de bonne heure early morning
débatnom debate
la débat est the debate is
débutantnom.masculin beginner
il est un débutant he is a beginner
décagonenom decagon
un décagone a dix a decagon has ten
Décembrenom December
Dimanche. Décembre 25, 1960 Sunday. December 25, 1960
décennienom decade
ce décennie this decade
déceptionnom disappointment
amour a déception love has disappointment
décèsnom death
place de décès place of death
décevoiract disappoint
je décevois I disappoint
déchetsnom waste
sa déchets her waste
déchireract tear
déchirez tear
déclarationnom.feminin statement
ell'écri une déclaration she records a statement
décolleract peel off
le chien décolle the dog peels off

décomposition^{nom.feminin} decay
 décomposition est mauvais decay is bad
déduire^{act} deduct
 déduisez un deduct one
défaite^{nom} defeat
 ma défaite my defeat
déféquer^{act} defecate
 nous déféquons we defecate
défi^{nom.masculin} challenge
 un défi bon a good challenge
défiler^{act} march
 la soldat défilera the soldier will march
dégonfler^{act} deflate
 elles dégonflent they deflate
dégoûtant^{adj} disgusting
 la sol est dégoûtant the floor is disgusting
dehors^{adv} outside
 promenade extérieur stroll outside
délicieux^{adj.masculin} delightful
 travail délicieux delightful work
demande^{nom} demand
 demande et offre demand and supply
demander^{act} ask
 demander Kofi to ask Kofi
demander^{act} request
 tu demandes you request
dent^{nom} tooth
 dent blanc white tooth
dentifrice^{nom.masculin} toothpaste
 brosse à dents et dentifrice toothbrush and tooth-paste
dépassé^{adj.masculin} outdated
 camion dépassé outdated lorry
déranger^{act} bother
 le chien dérange the dog bothers
déranger^{nom.masculin} bother
 ton déranger your bother
dernier^{adj.masculin} last
 il est dernier he is last
dernier-né^{nom} lastborn
 ta dernier-né your lastborn
des choses^{nom.pluriel} things
 tes des choses your things
désert^{nom} desert
 sa désert her desert
désir^{nom} desire
 ta désir your desire

desséché^{adj} parched
 sa peau est desséché his skin is parched
desséché^{adj} thirsty
 il est desséché it is thirsty
desserrer^{act} loosen
 nous desserrons we loosen
dessin animé^{nom.masculin} cartoon
 ton dessin animé your cartoon
dessiner^{act} draw
 dessinez un oiseau draw a bird
détermination^{nom} determination
 sa détermination her determination
détruire^{act} destroy
 elles détruisent le livre they destroy the book
dette^{nom} debt
 ta dette your debt
deux^{adj} two
 il est deux it is two
deux personnes^{nom} two persons
 ma deux personnes my two persons
devant^{pre} in front
 allez dans avant go in front
développement^{nom} development
 ma développement my development
devenir^{act} become
 devenir riche to become rich
devoir^{act} owe
 I owe you
diable^{nom} devil
 sa diable her devil
diamant^{nom} diamond
 un diamant blanc a white diamond
dictionnaire^{nom} dictionary
 image dictionnaire image dictionary
dieu^{nom} god
 dieu fiable dependable god
différent^{adj} different
 nous sommes différent we are different
difficile^{adj} difficult
 le travail est difficile the work is difficult
difficile^{adj} hard
 le travail est difficile the work is hard
difficilement^{adv} hard

difficulté^{nom} trouble
 difficulté et douleur trouble and pain
difficultés^{nom} hardship
 difficultés grand great hardship

Dimanche^{nom} Sunday

sa Dimanche her Sunday

dîme^{nom} tithe

payez ta dîme pay your tithe

dinde^{nom} turkey

la viande de un dinde the meat of a turkey

dîner^{act} dine

tu dînes you dine

diplômé^{nom} graduate

ell'est un diplômé she is a graduate

dire^{act} speak

elle di she speaks

dire^{act} say

je disez I say

dire au revoir^{act} say goodbye

tu dis au revoir you say goodbye

diriger^{act} steer

tu diriges you steer

discipliner^{act} discipline

disciplinez ta enfant discipline your child

discorde^{nom} discord

ta discorde your discord

disgrâce^{nom.feminin} disgrace

honte et disgrâce shame and disgrace

disparaître^{act} disappear

le chien disparaît the dog disappears

disposition^{nom} disposition

ta disposition your disposition

diss^{nom} diss

ma diss my diss

distingué^{adj} distinguished

la famill'est distingué the family is distinguished

distribuer^{act} deliver

distribuez argent deliver money

divertir^{act} entertain

divertissez yourself entertain yourself

diviser^{act} divide

divisez le pain divide the bread

division^{nom} division

ma division my division

divorce^{nom} divorce

mariage et divorce marriage and divorce

dix^{adj} ten

dix ten

dix-huit^{adj} eighteen

dix-huit eighteen

dix-huitième^{adj.masculin} eighteenth

le chat dix-huitième the eighteenth cat

dix-neuf^{adj} nineteen

dix-neuf nineteen

dix-neuvième^{adj.masculin} nineteenth

le chien dix-neuvième the nineteenth dog

dix-sept^{adj} seventeen

il est dix-sept it is seventeen

doigt^{nom.masculin} finger

ton doigt your finger

dollar^{nom} dollar

sa dollar her dollar

domaine^{nom.masculin} realm

nouvelles du domaine news of the realm

donner^{act} give

donnez l'eau give the water

donner naissance^{act} birth

nous donnons naissance we birth

dormir^{act} sleep

tu dors you sleep

doucement^{adv} gently

douleur^{nom} pain

la douleur est où the pain is where

douleur^{nom} grief

douleur est grief is

doute^{nom} doubt

ell'a doutes she has doubts

doux^{adj} sweet

la thé est doux the tea is sweet

doux^{adj} soft

le pain est doux the bread is soft

doux^{adj.masculin} gentle

un langue doux a gentle tongue

douze^{adj} twelve

il est douze it is twelve

douzième^{adj.masculin} twelfth

la nuit douzième the twelfth night

drapeau^{nom.masculin} flag

drapeau jaune yellow flag

droit^{adj} right

nous allons droit we go right

droit^{adj} straight

la rue est droit the road is straight

droits^{nom} rights

tu as droits you have rights

du froid^{adj} cold

l'eau est du froid the water is cold

du vin^{nom} wine

nous boisons du vin we drink wine

duper^{act} deceive
nous dupons we deceive
durée^{nom} duration
forty-hour durée forty-hour duration
e-mail^{nom} email
imprimez l'e-mail print the email
eau^{nom} water
tu bois l'eau you drink the water
ebola^{nom} ebola
ebol'est un maladie ebola is a disease
écarlate^{adj} scarlet
un robe écarlate a scarlet dress
écart^{nom} gap
ell'a un écart belle she has a beautiful gap
échelle^{nom} ladder
échelle longue long ladder
école^{nom.masculin} school
ton école your school
économie^{nom} economy
l'économie de Afrique the economy of Africa
écorce^{nom} bark
écorce de un arbre bark of a tree
écouter^{act} listen
nous écoutons we listen
écrire^{act} record
nous écrisons un lettre we record a letter
Écriture^{nom} scripture
ma Écriture my scripture
écrivain^{nom} author
je suis un écrivain I am an author
écrou^{nom.masculin} nut
manger l'écrou eat the nut
écureuil^{nom} squirrel
un écureuil aime paume écrou a squirrel likes palm nut
éducation^{nom} education
santé et éducation health and education
efficacité^{nom.feminin} efficiency
l'efficacité de un moteur the efficiency of an engine
effort^{nom} effort
un effort bon a good effort
effrayant^{adj} scary
la film est effrayant the film is scary
effrayer^{act} frighten
effrayez mal gens frighten evil people
effrayer^{act} scare
nous effrayons we scare

église^{nom} church
église et pays church and country
égoïsme^{nom} selfishness
égoïsme est selfishness is
élastique^{adj} elastic
la chaîne est élastique the string is elastic
électricité^{sci} electricity
nous vouloissons électricité we want electricity
électrique^{adj} electric
lumière électrique electric light
électron^{sci} electron
la charge électrique de un électron est -1 the electric charge of an electron is -1
électronique^{adj.masculin} electronic
un machine électronique an electronic machine
elle^{pro} she
elle mange la nourriture she eats the food
elle^{pro.feminin} her
montrer elle show her
elles^{pro} they
elles mangent la nourriture they eat the food
éloge^{nom} praise
elle mérite éloge she deserves praise
émerveillement^{nom} wonder
émerveillement et amour wonder and love
employeur^{nom.masculin} employer
ton employeur est bon your employer is good
emprunter^{act} borrow
empruntez argent borrow money
en avant^{adv} forward
aller en avant go forward
en bas^{adv} down
allez down go down
en dessous de^{adv} under
s'asseoir en dessous de l'arbre sit under the tree
en haut^{adv} up
regardez up look up
en retard^{adv} late

enceinte^{adj.feminin} pregnant
un femme enceinte a pregnant woman
enclume^{nom} anvil
marteau et enclume hammer and anvil
encore^{adv} still
still doing still doing
encore^{adv} again
voyez see

encouragement^{nom} encouragement

encouragement et joie encouragement and joy

encourager^{act} encourage

encourager encourage

encre^{nom} ink

encre ink

énergie^{sci} energy

masse et énergie mass and energy

enfance^{nom} childhood

ma enfance my childhood

enfant^{nom} child

ma enfant my child

enfant de mêmes parents^{nom} sibling

ma enfant de mêmes parents my sibling

énigme^{nom} riddle

ma énigme my riddle

enlever^{act} remove

tu enleves you remove

ennéagone^{nom} nonagon

un ennéagone a neuf a nonagon has nine

ennuyeuse^{adj.masculin} boring

l'histoire est ennuyeuse the story is boring

ennuyeux^{adj} annoying

il est ennuyeux it is annoying

énorme^{adj.masculin} huge

un bâtiment énorme a huge building

enquête^{nom} investigation

they will do an investigation

enregistrer^{act} save

enregistrez it save it

enseignant^{nom} professor

je suis un enseignant I am a professor

enseigner^{act} teach

ell'enseigne she teaches

ensemble^{adv} together

ensoleillé^{adj} sunny

un jour ensoleillé a sunny day

entendre^{act} hear

ell'entendsez la sifflet she hear the whistle

enterrement^{nom} funeral

sa enterrement her funeral

enterrer^{act} bury

je enterre I bury

entier^{adj.masculin} whole

l'argent est entier who is the moneyle

entourer^{act} surround

tu entoures you surround

entraîneur^{nom} coach

ma entraîneur my coach

entrée^{nom} entry

un entrée nouveau a new entry

entreprise^{nom} company

un entreprise petit a small company

entrer^{act} enter

envie^{nom.masculin} envy

avidité et envie gred and envy

envoyer^{act} send

envoyez me send me

épaule^{nom.feminin} shoulder

sa épaule her shoulder

éponge^{nom} sponge

ma éponge my sponge

époux^{nom.masculin} spouse

mon époux my spouse

épuiser^{act} deplete

nous épuisons we deplete

équipe^{nom} team

ma équipe my team

Erythrée^{nom} Eritrea

ta Erythrée your Eritrea

escalier^{nom} stair

escargot^{nom} snail

je mangez escargots I eat snails

esclave^{nom} slave

ma esclave my slave

espion^{nom} spy

il est un espion he is a spy

espionnage^{nom} espionage

espionnage films espionage films

espionner^{act} spy

nous espionnons we spy

espoir^{nom} hope

je avez espoir I have hope

esprit^{nom.masculin} mind

son esprit pense une idée her mind thinks an idea

esprit^{nom.masculin} spirit

il a un esprit fort he has a strong spirit

essayer^{act} try

essayez again try again

essuyer^{act} wipe

ell'essuye she wipes

est^{nom} east
allez est go east
estimer^{act} estimate
estimez ta hauteur estimate your height
estomac^{nom} belly
estomac grand big belly
et^{cjn} and
Kofi et Ama Kofi and Ama
étage^{nom} class
il est dans étage he is in class
étaler^{act} spread out
il étale he spreads out
état^{nom} state
ma état my state
éteindre^{act} turn off
tu éteinds you turn off
éteindre^{act} switch off
tu éteinds you switch off
éternel^{adj} eternal
vie éternel eternal life
éternité^{nom} eternity
sa éternité her eternity
éternuer^{act} sneeze
nous éternuons we sneeze
Ethiopie^{nom} Ethiopia
sa Ethiopie her Ethiopia
étoile^{nom.feminin} star
le soleil est une étoile the sun is a star
étranger^{nom} foreigner

étranger^{nom} stranger
ta étranger your stranger
être^{act} be
tu es un personne important you are an important person
être^{nom.masculin} being
humain être human being
être d'accord^{act} agree
il est d'accord he agrees
être jaloux^{act} be jealous
ell'est jaloux she is jealous
étudiant^{nom} student
ma étudiant my student
eux-mêmes^{pro} themselves
elles aiment eux-mêmes they love themselves
éveiller^{act} awaken
nous éveillons we awaken

événement^{nom.masculin} event
son événement her event
évêque^{nom} bishop
ell'est un évêque she is a bishop
évier^{nom} sink
vidangez l'évier drain the sink
éviter^{act} avoid
éviter mal avoid evil
exam^{nom} exam
l'exam est facile the exam is easy
excusez moi^{exc} excuse me

exemple^{nom} example
un exemple bon a good example
expérience^{nom} experience
ell'a expérience she has experience
expliquer^{act} explain
je explique I explain
exploser^{act} explode
la bombe explosez the bomb explode
extension^{nom} extension
maison extension house extension
extérieur^{nom.masculin} outside
allez extérieur go outside
exulter^{act} exult
exulter exult
fable^{nom} fable
sa fable her fable
facile^{adj} easy
le travail est facile the work is easy
simple^{adj} basic
il est simple it is basic
facture^{nom.feminin} bill
sa facture her bill
faible^{adj} weak
je suis faible I am weak
faiblesse^{nom} weakness
dans sa faiblesse in her weakness
faim^{nom} hunger
faim et soif hunger and thirst
faire^{act} do
le chien fait the dog does
faire^{act} make
faites nourriture make food
faire confiance^{act} trust
je fais confiance I trust
falsification^{nom} falsification
sa falsification her falsification

familier[adj] familiar
un animal familier a familiar animal
fantôme[nom] ghost
je voyez un fantôme I see a ghost
fardeau[nom] burden
ma fardeau my burden
farine[nom] flour
maïs farine corn flour
faucon[nom.masculin] falcon
mon faucon my falcon
faucon[nom] hawk
un faucon et un poulet a hawk and a chicken
faute[nom] lapse
ma faute my lapse
favoritisme[nom] favouritism
ma favoritisme my favouritism
félicitations[nom] congratulations
félicitations et bien fait congratulations and well done
femelle[nom] female
ma femelle my female
femelle[adj.masculin] female
un enfant femelle a female child
femme[nom] wife
ma femme et ma enfant my wife and my child
femme[nom] woman
un femme joli a pretty woman
femme de ménage[nom] maid
ell'est un femme de ménage she is a maid
fenêtre[nom] window
ouvrir la fenêtre open the window
ferme[nom.feminin] farm
cacao ferme cocoa farm
fermement[adv] tightly
tenissez il hold it
fermer[act] close
fermer la porte close the door
fermer[act] shut
fermez la porte shut the door
fertile[adj] fertile
terre fertile fertile land
fesses[nom] buttocks
fesses grand big buttocks
festival[nom] festival
sa festival her festival
fête[nom] party
ta fête your party

fétiche[nom] fetish
ce vill'a un fétiche this town has a fetish
feu[nom] fire
sa feu her fire
feuillage[nom] foliage
coupez la feuillage cut the foliage
feuille[nom] leaf
feuille vert green leaf
Février[nom] February
Dimanche. Février 14, 1960 Sunday. February 14, 1960
fichier[nom] file
ordinateur fichier computer file
fierté[nom] pride
sa fierté his pride
fièvre[nom] fever
ell'a un fièvre she has a fever
fille[nom.feminin] girl
fille grande tall girl
fille[nom.feminin] daughter
ma fille my daughter
film[nom] film
cast de un film cast of a film
fils[nom] son
ma fils my son
fin[nom] end
ma fin my end
finir[act] finish
finir le travail to finish the work
fléau[nom] plague

flèche[nom.feminin] arrow
arc et flèche bow and arrow
flegme[nom] phlegm
essuyez la flegme wipe the phlegm
fleur[nom] flower
la fleur est blanc the flower is white
flûte[nom] flute
ma flûte my flute
foi[nom] faith
foi et paix faith and peace
foie[nom] liver
un chien a un foie a dog has a liver
fois[nom] times
fois dix ten times
folie[nom] folly
sa folie her folly

folle^{adj} foolish
un histoire folle a foolish story
fondation^{nom} foundation
fondation de la maison foundation of the house
football^{nom} soccer
ta football your soccer
force^{nom} strength
force et puissance strength and authority
force^{act} force
je force I force
force^{nom} force
ma force my force
forêt^{nom.feminin} forest
sa forêt her forest
forme^{nom} shape
la forme de la maison the shape of the house
fort^{adj} strong
un femme fort a strong woman
forteresse^{nom} fortress
dieu est ma forteresse god is my fortress
fosse^{nom} pit
creusez un fosse dig a pit
foudre^{nom} lightning
foudre et tonnerre lightning and thunder
fouet^{nom.masculin} whip
cheval fouet horse whip
foulard^{nom} headscarf
ma foulard my headscarf
foule^{nom} crowd
noisy foule noisy crowd
fourchette^{nom} fork
fourchette et couteau fork and knife
fourmi^{nom} ant
un fourmi rouge a red ant
fourmilière^{nom} anthill
un fourmilière grand a tall anthill
fourmis^{nom} ants

frais^{adj} fresh
l'eau est frais the water is fresh
français^{nom} French
ma français my French
France^{nom.feminin} France
ta France your France
franchement^{adv} frankly
disez il say it
frapper^{act} pound
je frappez fufu I pound fufu

frapper^{act} hit
il frappe he hits
frein^{nom} brake
frein de un voiture brake of a car
freiner^{act} brake
je freine I brake
frère^{nom.masculin} brother
son frère her brother
friction^{nom} friction
friction venissez friction come
frire^{act} fry
elle fri she fries
fromage^{nom} cheese
fromage bleu blue cheese
front^{nom} forehead
regardez à sa front look at her forehead
fruit^{nom} fruit
nous mangeons fruit we eat fruit
frustration^{nom.feminin} frustration
quelques frustration est bon some frustration is good
fufu^{nom} fufu
mangez fufu eat fufu
fumée^{nom} smoke
rotez fumée belch smoke
fusée^{nom.feminin} rocket
nous construirons une fusée grand we will build a big rocket
GaDangme^{nom} GaDangme
ma GaDangme my GaDangme
gagner^{act} win
tu gagnes you win
gallon^{nom} gallon
un gallon de eau a gallon of water
garage^{nom} garage
voiture garage car garage
garçon^{nom.masculin} boy
le garçon est the boy is
garçon^{nom} waiter
il est un garçon he is a waiter
garder^{act} guard
gardez la maison guard the house
garder^{act} keep
gardez la change keep the change
gare^{nom} station
train gare train station
gaspillé^{adj} wasted
nourriture gaspillé wasted food

gâteau[nom.masculin] cake
gâteau et du vin cake and wine
gauche[adj] left
nous allons gauche we go left
Gbe[nom] Gbe
ta Gbe your Gbe
géant[nom] giant
ta géant your giant
géant[adj] giant
il est un homme géant he is a giant man
gelé[adj.masculin] freezing
l'eau est gelé the water is freezing
gener[act] annoy
elle gene she annoys
générosité[nom] generosity
ta générosité your generosity
génial[adj] awesome
dieu génial awesome god
genou[nom] knee
ta genou your knee
gens[nom] people
ta gens your people
gentil[adj.masculin] kind
amour est gentil love is kind
gérer[act] manage
je gére I manage
gestionnaire[nom] manager
un gestionnaire bon a good manager
Ghana[nom] Ghana
nous aimons Ghana we love Ghana
gifler[act] slap
giflez him slap him
gingembre[nom] ginger
gingembre soupe ginger soup
ginseng[nom] ginseng
ginseng est un plante ginseng is a plant
girafe[nom.feminin] giraffe
une girafe est un animal a giraffe is an animal
globe oculaire[nom] eyeball
œil et globe oculaire eye and eyeball
gloire[nom] glory
gloire de humanité glory of humankind
glorifier[act] glorify
je glorifie Dieu I glorify God
glouton[nom] glutton
il est un glouton he is a glutton
glouton[adj.masculin] greedy
imbécile glouton greedy fool

gobelet[nom.masculin] beaker
son gobelet her beaker
gong gong[nom] gong gong
ma gong gong my gong gong
gorge[nom] throat
sa gorge her throat
gourvenante[nom.feminin] housekeeper
tu as besoin de une gourvenante you need a housekeeper
goût[act] taste
goût la nourriture taste the food
goutte[nom] drop
ta goutte your drop
gouvernance[nom] governance
gouvernance bon good governance
gouvernement[nom] government
ta gouvernement your government
gouverner[act] govern
gouvernez Ghana govern Ghana
gouverneur[nom] governor
ell'est la gouverneur she is the governor
goyave[nom] guava
la goyave est doux the guava is sweet
grace[nom] grace
la grace de dieu the grace of god
graine[nom] seed
graine orange trois three orange seed
graisse[nom] grease
graisse grease
graisse[adj] fat
graisse fat
gramme[nom] gramme
sa gramme her gramme
grand[adj] great
Dieu est grand God is great
grand[adj] big
un montagne est grand a mountain is big
grand[adj.feminin.masculin] tall
l'arbre est grand the tree is tall
grand-mère[nom] grandma
ma grand-mère my grandma
grand-père[nom] grandfather
ma grand-père my grandfather
grandir[act] age
tu grandis you age
gratter[act] scrape
tu grattes you scrape

gratuit^{adj} free
nourriture gratuit free food
gravir^{act} climb
il gravit l'arbre he climbs the tree
grenouille^{nom} frog
un grenouill'aime eau a frog likes water
gris^{adj.masculin} gray
cheveux gris gray hair
grossesse^{nom} pregnancy
ma grossesse est facile my pregnancy is easy
groupe^{nom} gang
sa groupe her gang
groupe d'âge^{nom} age group
ma groupe d'âge my age group
guêpe^{nom} wasp
sa guêpe her wasp
guérir^{act} heal
guérissez maladie heal disease
guérison^{nom} healing
ta guérison your healing
guerre^{nom} war
ta guerre your war
guerre civile^{nom} civil war
ma guerre civile my civil war
guerrier^{nom} warrior
guerrier de antiquité warrior of antiquity
guerriers^{nom} warriors

guider^{act} guide
tu guides you guide
Guinée^{nom} Guinea
sa Guinée her Guinea
habitat^{nom} habitat
ta habitat your habitat
habiter^{act} live
tu habites you live
habitude^{nom} habit
habitude mauvais bad habit
haïr^{act} hate
tu haïr you hate
hamac^{nom} hammock
ta hamac your hammock
hanche^{nom} hip
ta hanche your hip
Haoussa^{nom} Hausa
je dis Haoussa I speak Hausa
harceler^{act} harass
ell'harcelait le chien she harassed the dog

hareng^{nom} herring
un hareng est un poisson a herring is a fish
haricot^{nom} bean
riz et haricots rice and beans
Harmattan^{nom} harmattan
Harmattan apporte poussière harmattan brings dust
hauteur^{nom} height
hauteur et largeur height and width
heh^{exc} heh
sorry, heh sorry, heh
hélicoptère^{nom.masculin} helicopter
son hélicoptère her helicopter
hémorragie^{nom} bleeding
hémorragie est mauvais bleeding is bad
herbe^{nom} grass
un vache mâchez herbe a cow chew grass
hérisson^{nom} hedgehog
sa hérisson her hedgehog
héritage^{nom} inheritance
prétendsez ta héritage claim your inheritance
herpès^{nom} herpes
herpès est un maladie herpes is a disease
heure^{nom} hour
ta heure your hour
hexagone^{nom} hexagon
un hexagone a six a hexagon has six
hiplife^{nom.masculin} hiplife
hiplife est musique hiplife is music
hippopotame^{nom} hippopotamus
un hippopotame a un estomac grand a hippopotamus has a big belly
hirondelle^{nom} swallow
un chat et un hirondelle a cat and a swallow
histoire^{nom} history
apprendsez histoire learn history
histoire^{nom} story
raconter un histoire to tell a story
hmph^{exc} hmph

holà^{exc} whoa

homard^{nom} lobster
je mangez homard I eat lobster
hommage^{nom.masculin} tribute
elles donnes un hommage they give a tribute
homme^{nom} male
ta homme your male

homme^{nom.masculin} man
un homme grand a tall man
honnêteté^{nom.feminin} honesty
honnêteté est bon honesty is good
honneur^{nom} honour
honneur et amour honour and love
honte^{nom} shame
honte et disgrâce shame and disgrace
hôpital^{nom} clinic
allez à un hôpital go to a clinic
hoquet^{nom} hiccups
ma hoquet my hiccups
horloge^{nom} clock
ta horloge your clock
hôtel^{nom} hotel
she sleeps at a hotel
houe^{nom} hoe
houe et coutelas hoe and cutlass
huile^{nom} oil
l'huile the oil
huile végétale^{nom} vegetable oil
ta huile végétale your vegetable oil
huit^{adj} eight
chiens huits eight dogs
huit jours^{nom} eight days
ta huit jours your eight days
huit personnes^{nom} eight persons
ma huit personnes my eight persons
huître^{nom} oyster
je mangez huître I eat oyster
humain^{nom} human
nous sommes humains we are humans
humain^{adj.masculin} human
nous sommes humain we are human
humanité^{nom.masculin} humankind
humanité sont bon humankind are good
humble^{adj.masculin} humble
personne humble humble person
humilité^{nom} humility
tu montrez humilité you show humility
hydrogène^{nom} hydrogen
hydrogène voiture hydrogen car
hyène^{nom} hyena
ma hyène my hyena
ici^{adv} here
cliquez ici click here
ici^{nom} here
ici et là here and there

Igbo^{nom} Igbo
ma Igbo my Igbo
igname^{nom} yam
cuisez l'igname cook the yam
il^{pro} it
il mange la nourriture it eats the food
il^{pro} he
il mange la nourriture he eats the food
île^{nom} island
Seychelles île Seychelles island
image^{nom} image
image belle beautiful image
imbécile^{nom} fool
sa imbécile her fool
immédiatement^{adv} immediately
coupez cut
impertinence^{nom} impertinence
ma impertinence my impertinence
important^{adj} important
tu es un personne important you are an important person
imprimer^{act} print
nous imprimons we print
imprimeur^{nom} printer
livre imprimeur book printer
inactif^{adj} inactive
il est inactif he is inactive
inconnu^{adj.masculin} unfamiliar
l'animal est inconnu the animal is unfamiliar
incroyable^{adj} amazing
l'histoire est incroyable the story is amazing
Inde^{nom} India
ell'aime Inde she loves India
indépendance^{nom} independence
indépendance jour independence day
indien^{adj.masculin} Indian
Océan Indien Indian Ocean
indigo^{adj} indigo
la chiffon est indigo the cloth is indigo
infertile^{adj.masculin} infertile
terre infertile infertile land
infini^{nom} infinity
infini êt un numéro infinity be not a number
infirmière^{nom} nurse
ell'est un infirmière she is a nurse
information^{nom.masculin} information
nous avons l'information we have the information

informatique^{nom} computing
sa informatique her computing
informer^{act} let ... know
je informe I let know
ingénieur^{nom} engineer
un ingénieur fait un outil an engineer makes a tool

ingrat^{adj} ungrateful
quelqu'un est ingrat somebody is ungrateful
inimitié^{nom} enmity
inimitié grand great enmity
inondation^{nom} flood
Accra inondation Accra flood
insulte^{nom} insult
insultes beaucoup many insults
insulter^{act} insult
le chien insulte the dog insults
insultes^{nom} insults
insultes inutile unnecessary insults
intégrer^{act} integrate
nous intégrons we integrate
intelligent^{adj.masculin} clever
il est intelligent it is clever
interdire^{act} forbid
interdire forbid
Internet^{nom} internet
Internet lien internet link
interrompre^{act} interrupt
interrompsez him interrupt him
inutile^{adj} unnecessary
insultes inutile unnecessary insults
Islam^{nom} Islam
ta Islam your Islam
islamique^{adj} Islamic
il est islamique it is Islamic
ivoire^{nom} ivory
ivoire collier ivory necklace
ivresse^{nom} drunkenness
ivresse et douleur drunkenness and pain
ivrogne^{nom} drunkard
il est un ivrogne he is a drunkard
jama^{nom} jama
nous chantons jama we sing jama
jamais^{adv} never
non, jamais no, never
jambe^{nom} leg
swollen jambe swollen leg

Janvier^{nom} January
Janvier est un mois January is a month
jardin^{nom} garden
notre jardin our garden
jaune^{adj} yellow
le drapeau est jaune the flag is yellow
je^{pro} I
je mange la nourriture I eat the food
je vais bien^{exc} I am well
je vais bien et merci I am well and thank you
Jésus^{nom.masculin} Jesus
son Jésus her Jesus
jeter^{act} discard
jetez le balle discard the ball
jeter^{act} throw away
je jete I throw away
jeter^{act} throw
elle jete she throws
jeu^{nom} game
sa jeu her game
jeu^{nom} play
ma jeu my play
Jeudi^{nom} Thursday
ta Jeudi your Thursday
jeune^{adj} young
personne jeune young person
jeûne^{nom} fasting
prière et jeûne prayer and fasting
jeune garçon^{nom} young boy
sa jeune garçon her young boy
jeune homme^{nom} young man
ma jeun homme my young man
jeune mariée^{nom} bride
jeune mariée bride
jeunesse^{nom} youth
ma jeunesse my youth
joie^{nom} joy
joie et paix joy and peace
joli^{adj.feminin.masculin} pretty
la fleur est joli the flower is pretty
jollof^{nom} jollof
jollof est nourriture jollof is food
jonction^{nom} intersection
sa jonction her intersection
jonque^{nom} junk
sa jonque her junk
joue^{nom.feminin} cheek
ma joue my cheek

jouer^{act} play
elle joue she plays
jour^{nom} day
jour et nuit day and night
journal^{nom} newspaper
sa journal her newspaper
journaliste^{nom} journalist
ta journaliste your journalist
juge^{nom} judge
ma juge my judge
jugement^{nom} judgement
ta jugement your judgement
Juillet^{nom} July
Vendredi. Juillet 01, 1960 Friday. July 01, 1960
Juin^{nom} June
sa Juin her June
jumeau^{nom} twin
ell'est un jumeau she is a twin
jusqu'à^{pre} until
jusqu'à until
juste^{adj} just
il est juste it is just
juste^{adv} just
juste just
juste^{pre} just
juste just
justice^{nom} justice
liberté et justice freedom and justice
k^{pho} k
la son de k the sound of k
kenkey^{nom} kenkey
kenkey et ragoût kenkey and stew
kente^{nom} kente
kente chiffon kente cloth
Kenya^{nom} Kenya
sa Kenya her Kenya
kérosène^{nom} kerosene
bouteille de kérosène bottle of kerosene
khakhi^{nom} khakhi
khakhi short khakhi shorts
khebab^{nom} khebab
sa khebab her khebab
Kikongo^{nom} Kongo
il écri Kikongo he records Kongo
kilomètre^{nom} kilometer
sa kilomètre her kilometer
là^{nom} there
ici et là here and there

la^{det.feminin.masculin.pluriel} the
l'homme, la femme et l'enfant the man, the woman and the child
la chair de poule^{nom} goosebumps
ta la chair de poule your goosebumps
la chose the thing

la compassion^{nom} compassion
ell'a la compassion she has compassion
la diarrhée^{nom} diarrhoea
la diarrhée et fièvre diarrhoea and fever
la rébellion^{nom} rebellion
la la rébellion a the rebellion has
la sienne^{pro} hers
ce chose est la sienne this thing is hers
la vertu^{nom} virtue
ta la vertu your virtue
laboratoire^{nom} laboratory
un hôpital laboratoire a clinic laboratory
lac^{nom} lake
la lac a the lake has
laid^{adj} ugly
il est laid it is ugly
laine palmnut^{nom} palmnut wool
sa laine palmnut her palmnut wool
laisser^{act} leave
laissez il leave it
laisser^{act} let
laissez let
laisser tomber^{act} drop
laisser tomber le œuf to drop the egg
lait^{nom} milk
lait et sucre milk and sugar
lait maternel^{nom} breastmilk
boisez la lait maternel drink the breastmilk
lamentation^{nom.feminin} wailing
sa lamentation her wailing
lamentation^{nom} lamentation
ta lamentation your lamentation
lance^{nom} spear
lance un et pistolet un one spear and one gun
langue^{nom} language
langues beaucoups meny languages
langue^{nom} tongue
dog's langue dog's tongue
lapin^{nom} rabbit
un lapin blanc a white rabbit

large^{adj} wide
 rue large wide road
largeur^{nom} width
 hauteur et largeur height and width
largeur^{nom.feminin} breadth
 largeur et largeur breadth and width
larme^{nom} tear
 sa larme her tear
latrine^{nom} latrine
 sa latrine her latrine
laver^{act} launder
 je lave I launder
le midi^{nom} noon
 le midi a noon has
le pied^{nom} foot
 ma le pied my foot
le tiens^{pro} yours
 le livre est le tiens the book is yours
lécher^{act} lick
 nous léchons we lick
leçon^{nom} lesson
 apprendsez la leçon learn the lesson
lecture^{nom} reading
 répétez la lecture repeat the reading
léger^{adj} lightweight
 le livre est léger the book is lightweight
lent^{adj.feminin.masculin} slow
 la tortue est lent the tortoise is slow
lentement^{adv} slowly
 un tortue marche a tortoise walks
lentille^{nom} lens
 lentille de un appareil photographique lens of a
 camera
léopard^{nom.masculin} leopard
 un léopard a un queue a leopard has a tail
lèpre^{nom} leprosy
 lèpre est un maladie leprosy is a disease
lépreux^{nom} leper
 ma lépreux my leper
les notres^{pro} ours
 ce chose est les notres this thing is ours
lettre^{nom} letter
 sa lettre her letter
leur^{pos} their
 leur maison their house
leur^{pro} them
 montrez leur show them

lèvres^{nom} lip
 ma lèvres my lip
lézard^{nom.masculin} lizard
 un lézard mange herbe a lizard eats grass
liberté^{nom} liberty
 ta liberté your liberty
liberté^{nom} freedom
 liberté et justice freedom and justice
lien^{nom} link
 Internet lien internet link
ligne^{nom} line
 ta ligne your line
Lingala^{nom} Lingala
 sa Lingala her Lingala
lion^{nom.masculin} lion
 un lion a un queue a lion has a tail
liqueur^{nom} liquor
 versez un liqueur petit pour a little liquor
liquide^{adj} liquid
 eau liquide liquid water
lire^{act} read
 lire le livre read the book
lisser^{act} smoothen
 elle lisse she smoothens
lit^{nom.masculin} bed
 dormez le lit sleep the bed
litige^{nom} litigation
 il aime litige he likes litigation
livraison^{nom} delivery
 la livraison a the delivery has
livre^{nom.masculin} book
 ce livre this book
loge^{nom} lodge
 ma loge my lodge
logo^{nom} logo
 la logo de un affaires the logo of a business
loi^{nom} law
 la loi di the law says
longévité^{nom} longevity
 sa longévité her longevity
longue^{adj} long
 sa barbe est longue his beard is long
longueur^{nom} length
 hauteur, largeur et longueur height, width and
 length
louer^{act} praise
 tu loues you praise

loup^{nom} wolf
ma loup my wolf
lourd^{adj} heavy
la pierre est lourd the stone is heavy
Luganda^{nom} Luganda
ta Luganda your Luganda
lui^{pro} him
montrer lui show him
lui-même^{pro} himself
il respect lui-même he respects himself
lumière^{nom} light
lumière de la ciel light of the sky
Lundi^{nom} Monday
sa Lundi her Monday
lune^{nom.feminin} moon
la lune et le soleil the moon and the sun
lunettes^{nom} spectacles
il a besoin de lunettes nouveau he needs new spectacles
Luwo^{nom} Luwo
ma Luwo my Luwo
luxe^{nom} luxury
je voyez luxe I see luxury
ma^{pos.feminin.masculin.pluriel} my
ma maison my house
mâcher^{act} chew
nous mâchons we chew
machine^{nom} machine
machine nouveau new machine
mâchoire^{nom} jaw
ma mâchoire my jaw
Madame^{nom} madam
Madame Mary madam Mary
magazine^{nom} magazine
un magazine nouveau a new magazine
Mai^{nom} May
ma Mai my May
main^{nom} hand
sa main her hand
maintenant^{cjn} now

maintenant^{adv} now
allez now go now
maintenir^{act} maintain
il maintenit un maison he maintains a house
mais^{cjn} but
elle mange nourriture mais il boi eau she eats
food but he drinks water

maïs^{nom} corn
maïs et arachide corn and groundnut
maison^{nom} home
ta maison your home
maison^{nom} house
la maison the house
maison du parlement^{nom} parliament
ta maison du parlement your parliament
maître^{nom} master
maître Kofi master Kofi
maîtresse^{nom} mistress
maître et maîtresse master and mistress
majeur^{adj.masculin} major
un ville majeur a major town
mal^{nom} evil
quel mal est which evil is
mal de tête^{nom} headache
mal de tête et fièvre headache and fever
maladie^{nom} disease
guérissez maladie heal disease
mâle^{adj.masculin} billy
un enfant mâle a billy child
malédiction^{nom} curse
un prière et un malédiction a prayer and a curse
Malgache^{nom} Malagasy
ta Malgache your Malagasy
malheur^{nom} misfortune
sa malheur her misfortune
manchot^{nom.masculin} penguin
un manchot est un animal a penguin is an animal

manger^{act} eat
je mange I eat
mangue^{nom} mango
la mangue a the mango has
manière^{nom} manner
sa manière est amusant his manner is amusing
manioc^{nom.masculin} cassava
plantain et manioc plantain and cassava
manquer^{act} miss
je manquez maison I miss home
manteau^{nom.masculin} coat
mon manteau my coat
marché^{nom} market
allez à marché go to market
marcher^{act} walk
marcher lentement to walk slowly

Mardi^{nom} Tuesday
ma Mardi my Tuesday
mari^{nom} husband
j'aime ma mari I love my husband
mariage^{nom} marriage
mariage bon good marriage
mariage^{nom} wedding
ta mariage your wedding
marié^{nom} bridegroom
sa marié her bridegroom
marier^{act} marry
mariez me marry me
Mars^{nom} March

marsouin^{nom} porpoise
ta marsouin your porpoise
marteau^{nom} hammer
sa marteau her hammer
masse^{sci} mass
masse et énergie mass and energy
mastiquer^{act} masticate
un vache mastique herbe a cow masticates grass
matelas^{nom} mattress
un mateles nouveau a new mattress
mathématiques^{nom} mathematics
ell'enseigne mathématiques she teaches mathematics
matin^{nom} morning
matin de bonne heure early morning
mauvais^{adj} bad
un chose mauvais a bad thing
maximum^{adj} maximum
montant maximum maximum amount
méchanceté^{nom} wickedness
ta avarice et ta méchanceté your stinginess and your wickedness
méchant^{adj} wicked
l'animal est méchant the animal is wicked
médecin^{nom} doctor
ma médecin est nouveau my doctor is new
médecine^{nom} drug
médecine amer bitter drug
mélanger^{act} mix
elle mélange she mixs
melon^{nom.masculin} melon
melon vert green melon
membre^{nom.masculin} member
membre de l'équipe member of the team

mémoire^{nom.feminin} memory
ordinateur mémoire computer memory
mémorisation^{nom} memorization
quelques mémorisation est bon some memorization is good
mémoriser^{act} memorize
to mémorisez to memorize
menace^{nom} threat

mendier^{act} beg
je mendie I beg
mensonge^{nom} lie
il est un mensonge it is a lie
menteur^{nom} liar
sa menteur her liar
mentir^{act} lie

menton^{nom.masculin} chin
tu tenis ton menton you hold your chin
menuiserie^{nom} carpentry
elle connaît menuiserie she knows carpentry
mépris^{nom} contempt
ta mépris your contempt
merci^{exc} thanks
merci Mandela thanks Mandela
merci^{exc} thank you
merci, merci thank you, thank you
Mercredi^{nom} Wednesday
ma Mercredi my Wednesday
mère^{nom} mother
ma mère my mother
mériter^{act} deserve
je mérite I deserve
message^{nom} message
ma message my message
messager^{nom} courier
la messager arrivez the courier arrive
messagers^{nom} messengers
la messagers avez the messengers have
mesurer^{act} measure
mesurez deux measure two
métal^{nom} metal
chapeau de métal hat of metal
mètre^{nom} meter
ma mètre my meter
mètre^{nom} metre
ta mètre your metre

mettre^{act} lay
she will lay on the ground
meurtre^{nom} murder
potins et meurtre gossip and murder
meurtrier^{nom} murderer
il est un meurtrier he is a murderer
miel^{nom} honey
miel est doux honey is sweet
mien^{pro} mine
le livre est mien the book is mine
mieux^{adj.masculin} better
il est mieux it is better
mieux^{adv} better
il chante mieux he sings better
mil^{nom} millet
mil bouillie millet porridge
mile^{nom} mile
sa mile her mile
milieu^{nom} centre
êtes dans la milieu are in the centre
mille^{adj} thousand
mille thousand
milliard^{adj.masculin} billion
un milliard a billion
milliers^{adj} thousands
il est milliers it is thousands
million^{adj} million
un million a million
mince^{adj} thin
la fill'est mince the girl is thin
mince^{adj} slim
l'homme est mince the man is slim
mineur^{adj} minor
un ville mineur a minor town
minute^{nom} minute
ta minute your minute
miroir^{nom} mirror
miroir grand big mirror
miséricorde^{nom} mercy
bonté et miséricorde goodness and mercy
missus^{nom} missus
missus Clinton missus Clinton
moderne^{adj} modern
langue moderne modern language
moi^{pro} me
moi et tu me and you
mois^{nom} month
elle commence ce mois she starts this month

moitié^{nom} half
un et moitié one and half
moment^{nom} moment
la moment est the moment is
monde^{nom.masculin} world
ton monde your world
moniteur^{nom} monitor
cœur moniteur heart monitor
Monsieur^{nom} sir
sa Monsieur her sir
montagne^{nom} mountain
montagne peak mountain peak
montant^{nom.masculin} amount
un montant de argent an amount of money
montrer^{act} show
nous montrons we show
morceau^{nom} lump
un morceau de or a lump of gold
morceau^{nom} morsel
morceaux deux two mouthfuls
mordant^{adv} pungently
odeur pungently smell pungently
mordre^{act} bite
le chien mord un bâton the dog bites a stick
mort^{adj} dead
un arbre mort a dead tree
mortier^{nom} mortar
pilon et mortier pestle and mortar
mosquée^{nom.feminin} mosque
une mosquée nouveau a new mosque
mot^{nom} word
ta mot your word
mot de passe^{nom} password
change mot de passe change password
moteur^{nom.masculin} engine
un moteur nouveau a new engine
mouche^{nom} housefly
a housefly can
mouche^{nom} fly
un mouche vole a fly flies
mouche à viande^{nom} blowfly
mouche à viande êtes ennuyeux blowfly are annoying
mouchoir^{nom} handkerchief
ma mouchoir my handkerchief
moudre^{act} grind
je mouds I grind

mouillé^{adj} wet
 couverture mouillé wet blanket
mourir^{act} die
 tout le monde mouriront everyone will die
moustique^{nom} mosquito
 un moustique a a mosquito has
mouton^{nom} sheep
 the sheep sleeps
multiplication^{nom} multiplication
 ta multiplication your multiplication
mur^{nom} wall
 s'asseoissez la mur sit the wall
mûrir^{act} ripen
 je mûris I ripen
musicien^{nom} musician
 sa musicien her musician
musique^{nom} music
 jeu musique play music
musulman^{nom} muslim
 un chrétien et un musulman a Christian and a muslim
nœud^{nom} knot
 sa nœud her knot
nager^{act} swim
 je nage I swim
nain^{nom} dwarf
 ma nain my dwarf
nation^{nom} nation
 ta nation your nation
nausée^{nom} nausea
 nausée et mal de tête nausea and headache
navire^{nom} ship
 un navire grand a big ship
négocier^{act} bargain
 nous négocions we bargain
neige^{nom} snow
 sa neige her snow
neigeux^{adj} rainy
 un jour neigeux a rainy day
neigeux^{adj.masculin} snowy
 aujourd'hui est neigeux today is snowy
nerveux^{adj.masculin} nervous
 un personne nerveux a nervous person
nettoyer^{adj.masculin} clean
 la maison est nettoyer the house is clean
neuf^{adj} nine
 neuf nine

neuf personnes^{nom} nine persons
 ma neuf personnes my nine persons
neutron^{sci} neutron

neveu^{nom} nephew
 ma neveu my nephew
nez^{nom.masculin} nose
 oreill'et nez ear and nose
nièce^{nom} niece
 ta nièce your niece
nier^{act} deny
 nous nions we deny
Niger^{nom} Niger
 ma Niger my Niger
Nigeria^{nom} Nigeria
 ma Nigeria my Nigeria
Noé^{nom.masculin} Noah
 mon Noé my Noah
noël^{nom.masculin} Christmas
 ma famill'aiment noël my family love Christmas
noir^{adj} black
 chiffon noir black cloth
noix de coco^{nom} coconut
 ma noix de coco my coconut
noix de cola^{nom} kolanut
 ta noix de cola your kolanut
nom^{nom} name
 ma nom my name
nom^{nom.masculin} noun
 la phrase a un nom the sentence has a noun
nombril^{nom.masculin} belly button
 mon nombril my belly button
nommer^{act} nominate
 le chien nomme the dog nominates
non^{exc} no
 je dis "non" I say "no"
nord^{nom} north
 allez nord go north
normal^{adj} normal
 comportement normal normal behaviour
Norvège^{nom} Norway
 ta Norvège your Norway
notre^{pos} our
 notre maison our house
nourriture^{nom} food
 manger nourriture to eat food
nous^{pro} us
 montrez nous show us

nous^{pro} we
nous mangeons la nourriture we eat the food
nous-mêmes^{pro} ourselves
nous aimons nous-mêmes we love ourselves
nouveau^{adj} new
famille nouveau new family
nouvelles^{nom} news
nouvelles du domaine news of the realm
Novembre^{nom} November
ma Novembre my November
novice^{nom} novice
il est un novice he is a novice
noyau^{sci} nucleus

noyer^{act} drown
elle noye she drowns
nuage^{nom.masculin} cloud
un nuage blanc a white cloud
nuageux^{adj} cloudy
un jour nuageux a cloudy day
nuit^{nom} night
la nuit de Lundi the night of Monday
numéro^{nom} number
numéro number
obscurité^{nom} darkness
nuit apporte obscurité night brings darkness
obstacle^{nom} obstacle
sa obstacle her obstacle
occupé^{adj} busy
il est occupé it is busy
océan^{nom} ocean
nous voyons l'océan we see the ocean
odeur^{nom} smell
je sentissez un odeur I sense a smell
offre^{nom} supply
demande et offre demand and supply
oh^{exc} oh

oignon^{nom.feminin} onion
une oignon rouge a red onion
oindre^{act} anoint
ell'oindsez ma tête she anoint my head
oiseau^{nom} bird
un oiseau vole a bird flies
okro^{nom} okra
okro soupe okra soup
ombre^{nom} shade
ta ombre your shade

oncle^{nom} uncle
notre oncle our uncle
ongle^{nom.feminin} nail
ongl'et marteau nail and hammer
onze^{adj} eleven
onze eleven
opposer^{act} oppose
je oppose l'idée I oppose the idea
oppression^{nom} oppression
sa oppression her oppression
opprimer^{act} oppress
tu opprimes you oppress
option^{nom} option
ma option my option
or^{nom} gold
parfum et or fragrance and gold
orange^{adj} orange
la lumière est orange the light is orange
orange^{nom} orange
sa orange her orange
ordinateur^{nom} computer
ordinateur clavier computer keyboard
ordures^{nom} rubbish
sa ordures her rubbish
oreille^{nom} ear
oreill'et nez ear and nose
oreillette^{nom} earpiece
oreillette nouveau new earpiece
organiser^{act} arrange

Oromo^{nom} Oromo
sa Oromo her Oromo
orteil^{nom} toe
orteil et talon toe and heel
os^{nom} bone
ma main a oss my hand has bones
ostentatoire^{adj} ostentatious
la robe est ostentatoire the dress is ostentatious
où^{adv} where
où where
oublier^{act} forget
tu oublies you forget
ouest^{nom} west
allez ouest go west
oui^{exc} yes
je dis oui I say yes
oui^{exc} aye
Aye! Silence! Aye! Silence!

ours^{nom.masculin} bear
Sisi Kisi est un ours Sisi Kisi is a bear
outil^{nom.masculin} tool
son outil her tool
ouvrir^{act} open
je ouvrissez la porte I open the door
ovaire^{nom} ovary
sa ovaire her ovary
oware^{nom} oware
ta oware your oware
oxygène^{nom} oxygen
oxygène est dans air oxygen is in air
pacifier^{act} pacify
pacifier pacify
pacifique^{adj.masculin} Pacific
Océan Pacifique Pacific Ocean
pain^{nom.masculin} bread
nous mangerons pain we will eat bread
paix^{nom} peace
la paix de Dieu the peace of God
paludisme^{nom} malaria
paludisme est un maladie malaria is a disease
panier^{nom.masculin} basket
il achete un panier he buys a basket
pantoufle^{nom} slippers
ta pantoufle your slippers
papaye^{nom} papaya
papaye et banane papaya and banana
papillon^{nom.masculin} butterfly
un papillon est belle a butterfly is beautiful
par hasard^{adv} by any chance
avez tu have you
parabole^{nom} parable
sa parabole her parable
paralysie^{nom} paraliesis
paralysie est un maladie paraliesis is a disease
parapluie^{nom} umbrella
s'asseoir en dessous de la parapluie sit under the umbrella
parce que^{cjn} because
elle danse parce que ell'aime dans she dances because she likes dancing
pardon^{nom} forgiveness
amour, acceptation et pardon love, acceptance and forgiveness
pardon^{exc} sorry
pardon, pardon sorry, sorry

pardonner^{act} forgive
pardonnez moi forgive me
parent^{nom.masculin} parent
mon parent my parent
parents^{nom} parents
sa parents his parents
paresseux^{adj} lazy
le chien est paresseux the dog is lazy
parfois^{adv} sometimes
nous boisons parfois we drink sometimes
parfum^{nom} fragrance
la parfum de beurre de karité the fragrance of sheabutter
parjure^{nom} perjury
parjure de tribunal perjury of court
parler^{act} talk
tu parles you talk
parmi^{pre} among
among gens among people
part^{nom} share
ta part your share
partager^{act} share
tu partages you share
partenaire^{nom} partner
ell'est ma partenaire she is my partner
partie^{nom} part
ma partie my part
partout^{pro} everywhere
partout est chaud everywhere is hot
pas^{adv} not
il est pas un serpent it is not a snake
pas cher^{adj} cheap
le pain est pas cher the bread is cheap
passeport^{nom.masculin} passport
ton passeport your passport
passer^{act} happen
elle passe she happens
passion^{nom.feminin} passion
ell'a passion she has passion
passoire^{nom} collander
utilisez la passoire use the collander
pastèque^{nom} watermelon
mangez la pastèque eat the watermelon
patate douce^{nom.feminin} sweet potato
sa patate douce her sweet potato
pâte^{nom} dough
il appuyez la pâte he press the dough

patiencenom patience
amour et patience love and patience
patientnom patient

patientadj.masculin patient
amour est patient love is patient
patriotismenom patriotism
il a patriotisme he has patriotism
patronnom.masculin boss
mon patron my boss
paumenom palm
un paume a palm
pauvreadj poor
un pays pauvre a poor country
pauvreténom poverty
pauvreté ou richesse poverty or wealth
payeract pay
je paye I pay
paysnom country
ta pays your country
peaunom.feminin skin
peau sec dry skin
péchénom.masculin sin
péché et pardon sin and forgiveness
pêcheurnom fisherman
il est un pêcheur he is a fisherman
pédophilenom pedophile
il est un pédophile he is a pedophile
peigneact comb
je peigne mes cheveux I comb my hair
peignenom comb
utilisez un peigne use a comb
peindreact paint
il peind la mur he paints the wall
peinturenom paint
peinture blanc white paint
peleract peel
nous pelons we peel
pellenom spade
ma pelle my spade
pendreact hang
pendsez il hang it
pénisnom penis
ma pénis my penis
penséesnom thought
sa pensées her thought
penseract think
je pense jour chaque I think every day

pentagonenom pentagon
un pentagone a cinq a pentagon has five
perceract pierce
percez ta oreille pierce your ear
perdreact lose
il perdsez sa voie he lose his way
pèrenom.masculin dad
ton père your dad
périodenom period
ta période your period
perlenom.masculin bead
son perle her bead
permanentadj permanent
le boulot est permanent the job is permanent
permettreact allow
permettsez them allow them
perroquetnom parrot
sa perroquet her parrot
personnenom person
personne important important person
personnelnom staff
wooden personnel wooden staff
peseract weigh
pesez ta enfant weigh your child
pesewanom pesewa
cedi un fait un pesewa cent one cedi makes a hundred pesewa
petnom fart
sa pet sentit her fart smells
petitadj small
un chose petit a small thing
petitadj smaller
maison petit smaller house
petitadj little
versez un liqueur petit pour a little liquor
petit déjeunernom.masculin breakfast
mon petit déjeuner my breakfast
petit filsnom.masculin grandson
mon petit fils my grandson
petit-enfantnom.masculin grandchild
ton petit-enfant your grandchild
petite fillenom.feminin granddaughter
notre petite fille our granddaughter
peunom little
ma peu my little
peu souventadv seldomly
elle venit peu souvent ici she comes seldomly here

Peul^{nom} Fula
Peul langue Fula language
peur^{nom} fear
peur a fear has
peut-être^{adv} maybe
peut-être maybe
philanthrope^{nom} philanthropist
ell'est un philanthrope she is a philanthropist
philosophe^{nom} philosopher
ell'est un philosophe she is a philosopher
philosophie^{nom} philosophy
ma philosophie my philosophy
photo^{nom} photograph
prendsez un photo take a photograph
phrase^{nom} sentence
ta phrase your sentence
physique^{nom} physics
sa physique her physics
pian^{nom} yaws
pian est un maladie yaws is a disease
piano^{nom} piano
ma piano my piano
picorer^{act} peck
elle picore she pecks
pièce de monnaie^{nom} coin
sa pièce de monnaie her coin
pierre^{nom} stone
ma pierre my stone
piéton^{nom} pedestrian
ta piéton your pedestrian
pigeon^{nom} pigeon
un pigeon est un oiseau a pigeon is a bird
pigfeet^{nom} pigfeet
pigfeet soupe pigfeet soup
pilier^{nom} pillar

pilon^{nom} pestle
pilon et mortier pestle and mortar
pincer^{act} pinch
tu pinces you pinch
pintade^{nom} guinea-fowl
sa pintade her guinea-fowl
pionnier^{nom} pioneer
ma pionnier my pioneer
pistolet^{nom} gun
un soldat a un pistolet a soldier has a gun
pitoyable^{adj} pitiful
l'enfant est pitoyable the child is pitiful

pizza^{nom} pizza
ma pizza my pizza
place^{nom} place
ta place your place
plage^{nom} beach
plage sable beach sand
plaideur^{nom} litigant
ell'est un plaideur she is a litigant
plaie^{nom} sore
sa plaie her sore
plaisir^{nom} pleasure
montrez ta plaisir how do you do sr pleasure
plan^{nom} blueprint
un pot et un plan a pot and a blueprint
planète^{nom.feminin} planet
terre est une planète earth is a planet
planifier^{act} plan
elles planifient they plan
plantain^{nom} plantain
plantain et manioc plantain and cassava
plante^{nom} plant
plante rouge red plant
planter^{act} plant
elle plante she plants
plastique^{adj} plastic
tasse plastique plastic cup
plateau^{nom} tray
ta plateau your tray
plein^{adj} full
seau plein full bucket
pleurer^{act} cry
elle pleure she cries
plier^{act} bend
pliez il bend it
plonger^{act} immerse
plongez lui immerse him
pluie^{nom.feminin} rain
l'agriculteur vouloit pluie the farmer wants rain
plume^{nom} feather
ma plume my feather
plus^{adj.masculin} more
nourriture plus more food
plus^{adv} more
manger plus to eat more
plus que^{pre} more than
elle mange plus she eats more
plus tard^{adv} later

plusieurs^{adj} several
plusieurs several
poche^{nom} pocket
sa poche her pocket
poème^{nom.masculin} poem
il écri un poème he records a poem
poids^{nom} weight
un poids lourd a heavy weight
poignarder^{act} stab
elle poignarde she stabs
poignet^{nom} wrist
tenissez sa poignet hold her wrist
poing^{nom} fist
ta poing your fist
pointeur^{nom} pointer
utilisez la pointeur use the pointer
poisson^{nom.masculin} fish
poisson est nourriture fish is food
poitrine^{nom} chest
poitrine cheveux chest hair
poitrine^{nom.feminin} breast
poitrine de homme breast of man
poivre^{nom} pepper
la poivre the pepper
police^{nom} police
police cinq five police
politique^{nom} politics
tu aimez politiques you like politicss
pomme^{nom} apple
mangez la pomme eat the apple
pont^{nom} bridge
nous construirons un pont we will build a bridge
porc^{nom} pork
porc et bœuf pork and beef
porc^{nom} pig
un porc rose a pink pig
porc-épic^{nom} porcupine
porc-épic trou porcupine hole
porcelet^{nom} piglet
sa porcelet her piglet
portable^{nom.masculin} laptop
mon portable my laptop
porte^{nom} door
fermez la porte close the door
porte-parole^{nom} spokesperson
la porte-parole de un chef the spokesperson of a chief

porter^{act} carry
tu portes le livre you carry the book
porter^{act} wear
portez vêtements wear clothes
portier^{nom} porter
la portier portez un boîte the porter carry a box
position^{nom} position
un position bon a good position
pot^{nom} pot
métal pot metal pot
pot^{nom} jar
ma pot my jar
pot-de-vin^{nom.masculin} bribe
il vouloit un pot-de-vin he wants a bribe
potins^{nom} gossip
potins est gossip is
pou^{nom} louse
ma pou my louse
pouce^{nom} thumb
utilisez ta pouce use your thumb
poudrière^{nom} powder-keg
ta poudrière your powder-keg
poulailler^{nom} coop
elle construi un poulailler she builds a coop
poulet^{nom.masculin} chicken
poulet viande chicken meat
poupée^{nom} doll
ma poupée my doll
pour^{pre} for
for ourselves for ourselves
pourpre^{adj} purple
la fleur est pourpre the flower is purple
pourquoi^{adv} why
why so? why so?
pourrir^{act} rot
tu pourris you rot
poursuivre^{act} pursue
poursuitez him pursue him
pourtant^{cjn} yet
le livre est grand the book is big
pousser^{act} push
je pousse I push
poussière^{nom} dust
poussière rouge red dust
pouvoir^{act} can
I can
prédicateur^{nom} preacher
ell'est un prédicateur she is a preacher

préface^{nom} preface
 livre préface book preface
premier-né^{nom} firstborn
 ma premier-né my firstborn
première^{adj.masculin} first
 l'enfant première the first child
prendre^{act} take
 nous prendsons we take
prendre^{act} get
 prendsez le livre get the book
préparation^{nom} preparation
 faites préparation make preparation
préparer^{act} prepare
 la prêtre préparera the pastor will prepare
près^{adv} near
 tirez pull
préserver^{act} preserve
 je préserve I preserve
président^{nom} president
 la président a the president has
président^{nom.masculin} chairman
 son président her chairman
présidente^{nom.feminin} chairwoman
 ma présidente my chairwoman
presque^{adv} almost
 presque ici almost here
presser^{act} squeeze
 pressez l'orange squeeze the orange
prêt^{nom} loan
 je avez besoin de un prêt I need a loan
prétendre^{act} claim
 tu prétends you claim
prêter^{act} lend
 prêtez moi lend me
prêter^{act} loan
 prêtez moi loan me
prêtre^{nom} pastor
 ma prêtre my pastor
prévoir^{act} foresee
 nous prévoissons we foresee
prier^{act} pray
 nous prions we pray
prière^{nom} prayer
 prière est bon prayer is good
priorité^{nom} priority
 ta priorité est que what is your priority
prison^{nom} jail
 allez à prison go to jail

prix^{nom} price
 la prix est que what is the price
prix^{nom} award
 ta prix your award
problème^{nom} problem
 ma problème my problem
proclamation^{nom} proclamation
 proclamation de la proclamation of the
procrastination^{nom} procrastination
 procrastination est procrastination is
produit^{nom} product
 faire un produit make a product
profit^{nom} profit
 faites profit make profit
profond^{adj} deep
 un trou profond a deep hole
progrès^{nom} advancement
 je voyez progrès I see advancement
projet^{nom} project
 ma projet my project
promenade^{nom} stroll
 prendsez un promenade take a stroll
promesse^{nom} promise
 ta promesse your promise
promettre^{act} promise
 nous promettsons we promise
prophète^{nom} prophet
 prophète puissant powerful prophet
propriétaire^{nom} owner
 la propriétaire de la voiture the owner of the car
propriétaire^{nom} proprietor
 ell'est un propriétaire she is a proprietor
prospérité^{nom} prosperity
 paix et prospérité peace and prosperity
protection^{nom} protection
 ta protection your protection
protéger^{act} protect
 protégez us protect us
proton^{sci} proton
 la charge électrique de un proton est +1 the electric charge of a proton is +1
proverbe^{nom.masculin} proverb
 apprendre un proverbe learn a proverb
public^{nom} public
 ma public my public
publicité^{nom} ad
 sa publicité her ad

puis[adv] then
puis then
puissance[nom] authority
force et puissance strength and authority
puissant[adj] powerful
le moteur est puissant the engine is powerful
puits[nom] well
sa puits her well
punaise de lit[nom] bedbug
ta punaise de lit your bedbug
punir[act] punish
punissez him punish him
pur[adj] pure
or pur pure gold
puzzle[nom] puzzle
ta puzzle your puzzle
python[nom] python
un python est un serpent a python is a snake
qualité[nom.feminin] quality
la qualité du livre the quality of the book
quand[cjn] when
il venissez he come
quantité[nom] quantity
quantité de la nourriture quantity of the food
quarante[adj] forty
quarante forty
quartier[nom] area
sa quartier her area
quatorze[adj] fourteen
quatorze fourteen
quatre[adj] four
il est quatre it is four
quatre-vingt[adj] eighty
il est quatre-vingt it is eighty
quatre-vingt dix[adj] ninety
quatre-vingt dix ninety
quatrième[adj.masculin] fourth
la fille quatrième the fourth girl
que[pro] what
amour est que what is love
que[cjn] that
un enfant que marche a child that walks
que[cjn] than
il est grand he is tall
quel[det] which
quel child? which child?
quelqu'un[pro] somebody
ell'aime quelqu'un she loves somebody

quelque chose[pro] something
elles vouloissent quelque chose they want something
quelque chose[nom] something
sa quelque chose her something
quelque part[pro] somewhere
nous irons quelque part we will go somewhere
quelques[det] some
quelques nourriture some food
querelle[nom] quarrel
un querelle grand a big quarrel
querelles[nom] squabbles
ma querelles my squabbles
question[nom] question
j'ai un question I have a question
question[nom] issue
question nouveau new issue
queue[nom] tail
un chat a un queue a cat has a tail
qui[pro] who
il est qui who is he
qui sont intensifiés rapidement[exc] that escalated quickly
ma ami, qui sont intensifiés rapidement my friend, that escalated quickly
quinze[adj] fifteen
quinze fifteen
quinzième[adj.masculin] fifteenth
la chanson quinzième the fifteenth song
quotidiennement[adv] daily
il venit he comes
racine[nom] root
racine de un arbre root of a tree
raconter[act] tell
tu racontes you tell
ragoût[nom] stew
faites ragoût make stew
raisin[nom] raisin
mangez la raisin eat the raisin
raison[nom] reason
ma raison my reason
ramasser[act] collect
je ramasse I collect
ramasser[act] pick up
je ramasse I pick up
ramper[act] crawl
la bébé rampe the baby crawls

rançon^nom ransom
 payez un rançon pay a ransom
rangée^nom row
 sa rangée her row
rap^nom.masculin rap
 rap musique rap music
rapide^adj fast
 un cheval vite a fast horse
rappeler^act remind
 tu rappeles you remind
rapport^nom report
 faites un rapport make a report
rareté^nom scarcity
 rareté de eau scarcity of water
rasoir^nom razor
 affilez la rasoir sharpen the razor
rat^nom rat
 un rat grand a big rat
rebelle^nom rebel

rebord^nom ledge
 dormez la rebord sleep the ledge
rechercher^act search
 recherchez sa maison search his house
rectangle^nom.masculin rectangle
 un rectangl'a quatre a rectangle has four
réduire^act decrease
 réduisez il decrease it
réflexion^nom reflection
 sa réflexion his reflection
refroidir^act cool
 nous refroidissons we cool
refuge^nom refuge
 notre refuge our refuge
regarder^act watch
 nous regardons we watch
regarder^act look
 regardez à le garçon look at the boy
règle^nom rule
 elle suiv la règle she follows the rule
régler^act settle
 réglez là settle there
rein^nom kidney
 un chat a un rein a cat has a kidney
reine^nom queen
 ell'est un reine she is a queen
rejeter^act reject
 je rejete I reject

réjouir^act rejoice
 réjouissez, je rejoice, I
relancer^act revive
 relancez yourself revive yourself
remercier^act thank
 nous remercions we thank
remplacer^act replace
 remplacez moi replace me
remplir^act fill
 remplissez it fill it
remuer^act stir
 remuez la bouillie stir the porridge
rémunération^nom compensation
 ta rémunération your compensation
renard^nom fox
 je vois un renard I see a fox
rencontrer^act meet
 rencontrez moi meet me
renouveau^nom revival
 renouveau a revival has
réparer^act fix
 elle réparera la voiture she will fix the car
repentance^nom repentance
 amour et repentance love and repentance
répéter^act repeat
 répétez la lecture repeat the reading
replier^act fold
 nous replions we fold
répondre^act answer
 nous répondsons we answer
réponse^nom answer
 ma réponse my answer
réseau^nom network
 la réseau the network
respect^nom respect
 amour et respect love and respect
respect^act respect
 je respect l'enfant I respect the child
respirer^act breathe
 tu respires you breathe
responsabilité^nom.feminin accountability
 responsabilité et responsabilité responsibility and
 accountability
restaurant^nom.masculin restaurant
 un restaurant nouveau a new restaurant
reste^nom remainder
 la reste de la nourriture the remainder of the food

rester^{act} remain
nous restons we remain
résurrection^{nom} resurrection
la résurrection de Christ the resurrection of Christ

retarder^{act} delay
il retarde he delays
rétirer^{act} withdraw
il rétire he withdraws
retour^{act} return
nous retour we return
réunion^{nom} meeting
annulez la réunion cancel the meeting
rêve^{nom} dream
ta rêve your dream
reveiller^{act} wake
je reveille I wake
révélation^{nom} revelation
ma révélation my revelation
révéler^{act} reveal
révélez la vérité reveal the truth
rêver^{act} dream
tu rêves you dream
rhum^{nom} rum

rhumatisme^{nom} rheumatism
rhumatisme est un maladie rheumatism is a disease
riche^{adj} rich
un pays riche a rich country
richesse^{nom} wealth
richesse ou pauvreté wealth or poverty
rideau^{nom.masculin} curtain
la fenêtre a besoin de un rideau the window needs a curtain
rien^{nom} nothing
je avez rien I have nothing
rire^{nom.masculin} laughter

rire^{act} laugh
nous risons we laugh
rival^{nom} rival
ell'est ma rival she is my rival
rivalité^{nom} rivalry
ma rivalité my rivalry
rivière^{nom} river
un rivière et la mer a river and the sea

riz^{nom} rice
riz et haricots rice and beans
robe^{nom} dress
robe bleu blue dress
robinet^{nom} tap
ouvrissez la robinet open the tap
rocher^{nom} rock
un rocher grand a big rock
roi^{nom} king
il est un roi he is a king
ronflement^{nom} snoring
ronflement bruyant loud snoring
ronfler^{act} snore
I ronflez I snore
rose^{adj} pink
la porc est rose the pig is pink
rosée^{nom} dew
matin rosée morning dew
roter^{act} belch
je rote I belch
rôtir^{act} roast
rôtissez un maïs petit roast a little corn
roue^{nom} wheel
ta roue your wheel
rouge^{adj} red
rouge red
rouleau de papier toilette^{nom} toilet roll
rouleau de papier toilette un one toilet roll
royaume^{nom} kingdom
la royaume de dieu the kingdom of god
rue^{nom} street
rue nouveau new street
rue^{nom} road
rue nouveau new road
ruisseau^{nom} brook
ta ruisseau your brook
ruisseau^{nom} stream
ma ruisseau my stream
ruse^{nom} trick

rusé^{adj} cunning
un femme rusé a cunning woman
s'accroupir^{act} squat
je s'accroupis I squat
s'appuyer sur^{act} lean on
s'appuyer sur moi lean on me
s'asseoir^{act} sit
s'asseoir ici sit here

s'il vous plaît[adv] please
 s'il vous plaît et merci please and thank you
sœur[nom] sister
 sa sœur his sister
sa[pos.feminin.masculin] his
 sa maison his house
sa[pos.feminin.masculin] her
 sa maison her house
sa[pro] its
 son maison its house
sable[nom] sand
 plage sable beach sand
sabotage[nom] sabotage
 sa sabotage her sabotage
sac[nom] bag
 tu voulois la sac you want the bag
sac[nom] sack
 sac de charbon de bois sack of charcoal
sagesse[nom] wisdom
 force et sagesse strength and wisdom
saigner[act] bleed
 je saigne I bleed
saint[adj.masculin] holy
 ce livre est saint this book is holy
saisir[act] grab
 saisissez sa main grab his hand
saison sèche[nom] dry season
 ta saison sèche your dry season
sale[adj] dirty
 robe sale dirty dress
saleté[nom] dirt
 saleté et maladie dirt and disease
salle[nom.feminin] living-room
 sa salle his living-room
salle de bain[nom] bathroom
 allez à la salle de bain go to the bathroom
salle de cours[nom.feminin] classroom
 la salle de cours est nettoyer the classroom is clean

salon[nom] hall
 un salon grand a big hall
saluer[act] greet
 saluez Ama greet Ama
salut[nom] salvation
 ta salut your salvation
salut[exc] hi

Samedi[nom] Saturday
 ma Samedi my Saturday
sang[nom] blood
 eau et sang water and blood
sans abri[adj] homeless
 un personne sans abri a homeless person
santé[nom] health
 nourriture donne santé food gives health
sauf[cjn] except
 except dieu except god
sauter[act] jump
 nous sautons we jump
sauterelle[nom] grasshopper
 fourmi et sauterelle ant and grasshopper
sauvage[adj] wild
 animal sauvage wild animal
sauver[act] rescue
 elle sauvera moi she will rescue me
savant[nom] savant
 ma savant my savant
savoir faire[nom.masculin] expertise
 ell'a savoir faire she has expertise
savon[nom.masculin] soap
 savon et eau soap and water
scarabée[nom.masculin] beetle
 un scarabée rouge a red beetle
scie[nom] saw
 sa scie her saw
se battre[act] fight
 elle se battre she fights
se disputer[act] argue
 nous se disputer jour chaque we argue every day

se lever[act] stand
 tu se lever you stand
se marier[act] wed
 elle se marier she weds
se perdre[act] get lost
 je se perdre I get lost
se plaindre[act] whine
 je se plaindre I whine
se raccorder[act] join
 mots se raccorder words join
se répandre[act] spread
 se répandre it spread it
se repentir[act] repent
 elle se repentir she repents

se soucier[act] care
tu se soucier you care
seau[nom.masculin] bucket
le seau est rouge the bucket is red
seau[nom] pail
seau et savon pail and soap
sec[adj] dry
la terre est sec the land is dry
sécher[act] dry
tu séches you dry
seconde[nom] second
sa seconde her second
secouer[act] quake
nous secouons we quake
secret[nom.masculin] secret
je avez un secret I have a secret
secteur[nom] sector
sa secteur her sector
seize[adj] sixteen
seize sixteen
seizième[adj.masculin] sixteenth
la maison seizième the sixteenth house
sel[nom] salt
sucre et sel sugar and salt
sélectionner[act] select
nous sélectionnons we select
semaine[nom] week
ce semaine this week
semelle[nom] sole
ma semelle my sole
semer[act] sow
semez un arbre sow a tree
sensationnel[exc] wow

sentiment[nom.masculin] emotion
joie est un sentiment joy is an emotion
sentir[act] feel
il sentit sa amour he feels her love
sentir[act] sense
je sentissez I sense
sentir[act] smell
je sentis I smell
séparer[act] split
séparez dans deux split in two
sept[adj] seven
sept seven
sept personnes[nom] seven persons
ta sept personnes your seven persons

septagon[nom] heptagon
un septagon a sept a heptagon has seven
Septembre[nom] September
sa Septembre her September
seringue[nom] syringe
ma seringue my syringe
serment[nom] oath
serment grand great oath
serpent[nom.masculin] snake
un serpent avo un jambe a snake have not a leg
service[nom] service
ta service est bon your service is good
serviette[nom] towel
serviette mouillé wet towel
serviteur[nom] servant
ma serviteur my servant
seulement[adj] only
seulement only
sexy[adj] sexy
un homme sexy a sexy man
Shona[nom] Shona
sa Shona her Shona
short[nom.masculin] shorts
khakhi short khakhi shorts
si[cjn] if

si ... alors[cjn] if ... then
si A alors B if A then B
siècle[nom] century
ce siècle this century
sifflet[nom] whistle
souffler la sifflet blow the whistle
signe[nom] sign
un signe de espoir a sign of hope
signifier[act] signify
nous signifions we signify
silence[nom] silence
ta silence your silence
silex[nom] flint
utilisez la silex use the flint
simple[adj] mere
humain simple mere human
singe[nom.masculin] monkey
un singe mange banane a monkey eats banana
singleton[nom] singleton

site Web[nom] website
ta site Web your website

six^{adj} six
six six
six personnes^{nom} six persons
ma six personnes my six persons
slavegirl^{nom} slavegirl
ta slavegirl your slavegirl
soie^{nom} silk
soie blanc white silk
soif^{nom} thirst
je sentissez soif I feel thirst
soin^{nom.masculin} carefulness
mon soin my carefulness
soir^{nom} evening
ce soir this evening
soixante^{adj} sixty
soixante sixty
soixante-dix^{adj} seventy
il est soixante-dix it is seventy
sol^{nom} floor
la sol the floor
soldat^{nom} soldier
la soldat et la police the soldier and the police
soleil^{nom.masculin} sun
le soleil et la lune the sun and the moon
solide^{adj} solid
eau solide solid water
solution^{nom.feminin} solution
nous avons une solution we have a solution
Somalie^{nom} Somalia
ta Somalie your Somalia
sombre^{adj} dark
la nuit est sombre the night is dark
sommeiller^{act} doze
je sommeille I doze
sommet^{nom} summit
montagne sommet mountain summit
somnolence^{nom.feminin} drowsiness
sa somnolence her drowsiness
son^{pro} his
ce chose est son this thing is his
son^{nom} sound
son bruyant loud sound
son^{pos} its
son maison its house
sorcellerie^{nom} witchcraft
practise sorcellerie practise witchcraft
sorcellerie^{nom} sorcery
practise sorcellerie practise sorcery

sorcier^{nom} wizard
il est un sorcier he is a wizard
sorcière^{nom} witch
ell'est un sorcière she is a witch
souche^{nom} stump
souche de un arbre stump of a tree
souchet^{nom} tigernut
sa souchet her tigernut
souci^{nom} worry
ta souci your worry
souffle^{nom} breath
un souffle de air a breath of air
souffler^{act} blow
tu souffles air you blow air
souffrance^{nom} suffering
ma souffrance my suffering
souffrir^{act} suffer
tu souffris you suffer
souhaitable^{adj} desirable
il est souhaitable it is desirable
souhaiter^{act} wish
elle souhaite she wishs
souiller^{act} defile
elle souille she defiles
soulever^{act} lift
je souleve I lift
soupe^{nom} soup
sa soupe her soup
soupir^{act} sigh
tu soupis you sigh
soupirs^{nom} sighing
ta soupirs your sighing
sourcil^{nom} eyebrow
œil et sourcil eye and eyebrow
sourire^{act} smile
nous sourisons we smile
souris^{nom} mouse
un souris grand a big mouse
souris^{sci} mouse
ordinateur souris computer mouse
sous-marin^{nom} submarine
un sous-marin nouveau a new submarine
soustraction^{nom} subtraction
sa soustraction her subtraction
soustraire^{act} subtract
soustraisez un subtract one
soutenir^{act} prop
soutenissez la porte prop the door

souvenir^{act} remember

moi souvenissez tu me remember you

souvent^{adv} often

elle she

spécial^{adj} special

jour spécial special day

spécifique^{adj} specific

il est spécifique it is specific

spectateur^{nom} spectator

ta spectateur your spectator

sponsor^{nom} sponsor

ta sponsor your sponsor

sport^{nom} sport

ell'aime sports she likes sports

stade^{nom.masculin} stadium

un stade nouveau a new stadium

stérile^{adj} barren

femme stérile barren woman

studio^{nom.masculin} studio

un musique studio a music studio

stupide^{adj.masculin} dumb

il est stupide it is dumb

stylo^{nom} pen

ta stylo your pen

succès^{nom} success

succès et bonheur success and happiness

sucer^{act} suck

un bébé suce lait a baby sucks milk

sucre^{nom} sugar

sucre et eau sugar and water

sud^{nom} south

allez sud go south

suie^{nom} soot

suie noir black soot

suivant^{adj.masculin} next

page suivant next page

suivre^{act} follow

suitez me follow me

support^{nom.masculin} bracket

ell'écri un support she records a bracket

sur^{pre} on

dormez la table sleep the table

surprise^{nom} surprise

surprise grand great surprise

Swahili^{nom} Swahili

Swahili langue Swahili language

symbole^{nom} symbol

symbole de puissance symbol of authority

ta^{pos.feminin.masculin.pluriel} your

ta maison your house

tabac^{nom} tobacco

fumée tabac smoke tobacco

tabac à priser^{nom} snuff

ta tabac à priser your snuff

table^{nom} table

chaise et table chair and table

tabouret^{nom} stool

s'asseoissez la tabouret sit the stool

taille^{nom} waist

ta taille your waist

talon^{nom} heel

orteil et talon toe and heel

tambour^{nom} drum

je entendsez la tambour I hear the drum

tandis que^{cjn} while

tante^{nom} aunt

notre tante our aunt

taper^{act} type

je tapez I type

tapis^{nom.masculin} carpet

tapis nouveau new carpet

tapis^{nom} mat

sa tapis her mat

taquiner^{act} tease

taquinez him tease him

tarentule^{nom} tarantula

un tarentule grand a large tarantula

taro^{nom.masculin} cocoyam

j'aimez taro I like cocoyam

taro feuilles^{nom.pluriel} cocoyam leaves

tes taro feuilles your cocoyam leaves

tas^{nom} heap

un tas de sable a heap of sand

tasse^{nom} cup

thé tasse tea cup

taxe^{nom} tax

nous payons la taxe we pay the tax

taxi^{nom} taxi

ma taxi my taxi

technique^{adj} technical

travail technique technical work

teigne^{nom} ringworm

il a teigne he has ringworm

télécharger^{act} download

télécharger la chanson download the song

téléphone^{nom} phone
 maison téléphone house phone
téléphoner^{act} phone
 tu téléphonez moi you phone me
télévision^{nom} television
 ma télévision my television
témoignage^{nom} testimony
 ta témoignage est que what is your testimony
témoin^{nom} witness
 ma témoin my witness
tempête^{nom} storm
 tempête de tonnerre storm of thunder
temple^{nom.masculin} temple
 un temple nouveau a new temple
temps^{nom} time
 la temps est the time is
tendance^{nom} trend
 un tendance bon a good trend
tenir^{act} hold
 tenir la bouteille hold the bottle
tenue^{nom} attire
 ta tenue est belle your attire is beautiful
termites^{nom} termite
 sa termites her termite
terre^{nom} earth
 terre bon good earth
terre^{nom} land
 achetez terre buy land
test^{nom} assessment
 la test est difficile the assessment is difficult
testament^{nom} testament
 testament nouveau new testament
tester^{act} test
 le chien teste the dog tests
testicule^{nom} testicle
 ta testicule your testicle
tête^{nom} head
 ta tête grand your big head
téter^{act} suckle
 tétez la poitrine suckle the breast
thé^{nom} tea
 la thé est doux the tea is sweet
tie-and-dye^{nom} tie-and-dye
 ta tie-and-dye your tie-and-dye
tigre^{nom} tiger
 un tigre grand a large tiger
timbre^{act} stamp
 elle timb she stamps

tirer^{act} pull
 nous tirons we pull
tirer^{act} shoot
 nous tirons we shoot
tiroirs^{nom} drawers
 ta tiroirs your drawers
tisserin^{nom} weaverbird
 ma tisserin my weaverbird
tissu^{nom} fabric
 sa tissu her fabric
titre^{nom} title
 la titre de un livre the title of a book
Togo^{nom} Togo
 ma Togo my Togo
toi^{pro} ye
 moi et toi me and ye
toi^{pro} you
 j'aimez toi I love you
toi même^{pro} yourself
 tu aimes toi même you love yourself
toile^{nom} canvas
 un toile grand a large canvas
toile^{nom.feminin} web
 la toile de un araignée the web of a spider
toilettes^{nom} toilet
 allez à la toilettes go to the toilet
tomate^{nom} tomato
 ta tomate your tomato
tombée de la nuit^{nom.feminin} nightfall
 aube et tombée de la nuit daybreak and nightfall

tomber^{act} fall
 je tombe I fall
tonnerre^{nom} thunder
 tempête de tonnerre storm of thunder
tortue^{nom} tortoise
 un tortue marche a tortoise walks
tôt^{adv} early
 venissez de bonne heure come early
total^{adj} total
 le montant total the total amount
totalement^{adv} totally
 il est it is
toucher^{act} touch
 elle touche she touches
toujours^{adv} forever
 ell'habitez she live

toujours^{adv} always
il est he is
toupie^{nom} spinning top

tousser^{act} cough
la bébé tousse the baby coughs
tout^{adj} entire
la maison tout the entire house
tout^{pro} everything
tout est nouveau everything is new
tout^{det} all
tout des choses all things
tout^{adj.masculin} all
cet est tout this is all
tout^{adj.masculin} any
livre tout any book
tout^{pro} all
tout sont noir all are black
tout à coup^{adv} suddenly
il venissez it come
tout le monde^{pro} everyone
tout le monde veniront everyone will come
tout-puissant^{adj} almighty
Dieu est tout-puissant God is almighty
Tout-puissant^{nom} Almighty
sa Tout-puissant her Almighty
toux^{nom} cough
il a un toux he has a cough
tradition^{nom.feminin} tradition
ta tradition your tradition
traduire^{act} translate
traduire Anglais à Akan to translate English to Akan

trahir^{act} betray
tu trahis you betray
train^{nom.masculin} train
un train nouveau a new train
traître^{nom} traitor
ta traître your traitor
transport^{nom.masculin} transportation
ell'a transport she has transportation
travail^{nom.masculin} work
le travail est bon the work is good
travail^{nom} working
travail est working is
travailler^{act} work
nous travaillons we work

traverser^{act} cross
tu traverses you cross
trébucher^{act} stumble
elles trébuchent they stumble
treize^{adj} thirteen
treize thirteen
treizième^{adj.masculin} thirteenth
la jour treizième the thirteenth day
tremblement de terre^{nom} earthquake
la tremblement de terre venit the earthquake comes

trembler^{act} tremble
tu trembles you tremble
trente^{adj} thirty
trente thirty
très^{adv} very
tu avez you have
très souhaitable^{adj} very desirable
il est très souhaitable it is very desirable
trésor^{nom} treasure
trésor grand great treasure
triangle^{nom.masculin} triangle
un triangl'a trois a triangle has three
tribunal^{nom} court
la tribunal de justice the court of justice
tricher^{act} cheat
elle triche she cheats
trillion^{adj.masculin} trillion
un trillion one trillion
trinité^{nom} trinity
trinité saint holy trinity
triplés^{nom} triplets
ma triplés my triplets
triste^{adj} sad
un visage triste a sad face
trois^{adj} three
trois three
trois personnes^{nom} three persons
sa trois personnes her three persons
tromperie^{nom} deception
tromperie et discorde deception and discord
trompette^{nom} trumpet
sa trompette her trumpet
trône^{nom} throne
sa trône her throne
trop^{adv} too much
il insultez he insult

troquer^{act} trade
 je troque I trade
trou^{nom} hole
 trou petit small hole
trouver^{act} find
 trouvez la mot find the word
tu^{pro} you
 tu manges la nourriture you eat the food
tuer^{act} kill
 nous tuons we kill
turbulent^{adj} turbulent
 un monde turbulent a turbulent world
tuyau^{nom} pipe
 tuyau eau pipe water
tweeter^{act} tweet
 un oiseau tweete a bird tweets
ukulélé^{nom} ukelele
 sa ukulélé her ukelele
un^{adj} one
 il est un it is one
un^{det.feminin.masculin} a
 un homme, un femme et un enfant a man, a woman and a child
unappreciativeness^{nom} unappreciativeness
 sa unappreciativeness her unappreciativeness
une personne^{nom} one person
 ta une personne your one person
union^{nom} union
 African union African union
unir^{act} unite
 nous unissons we unite
unité^{nom} unit
 ta unité your unit
unité^{nom} unity
 unité et paix unity and peace
université^{nom} university
 ta université your university
urine^{nom} urine
 l'urine the urine
uriner^{act} urinate
 tu urines you urinate
Ururimi^{nom} Ururimi
 ma Ururimi my Ururimi
utérus^{nom} womb
 l'utérus de un femme the womb of a woman
utilisateur^{nom} user
 ma utilisateur my user

utiliser^{act} use
 je utilise I use
vacciner^{act} vaccinate
 elle vaccine she vaccinates
vache^{nom} cow
 un vache mange herbe a cow eats grass
vagin^{nom} vagina
 ta vagin your vagina
vague^{nom} wave
vaillant^{adj} valiant
 il est vaillant it is valiant
valeur^{nom.feminin} value
 je comprends la valeur I understand the value
vallée^{nom} valley
 ta vallée your valley
varicelle^{nom} chickenpox
 varicell'est un maladie chickenpox is a disease
vase^{nom} vase
 argile vase clay vase
vautour^{nom.masculin} vulture
 ton vautour your vulture
véhicule^{nom} vehicle
 un véhicule nouveau a new vehicle
veine^{nom} vein
 sa veine his vein
vélo^{nom.masculin} bicycle
 vélo nouveau new bicycle
vendre^{act} sell
 elle vend she sells
Vendredi^{nom} Friday
 ma Vendredi my Friday
venin^{nom} venom
 venin de un serpent venom of a snake
venir^{act} come
 venissez here! come here!
vent^{nom} wind
 la vent est the wind is
venteux^{adj} windy
 un jour venteux a windy day
ventilateur^{nom} fan
 ventilateur électrique electric fan
ver^{nom.masculin} worm
 ver, où worm, where
véranda^{nom} verandah
 ta véranda your verandah
verbe^{nom.masculin} verb
 la phrase a un verbe the sentence has a verb

verdâtre^{adj} greenish
maison verdâtre greenish house
vérité^{nom} truth
elle disez la vérité she speak the truth
verre^{nom} tumbler
verre un de eau one tumbler of water
vers le bas^{adv} downward

verser^{act} pour
versez eau pour water
verset^{nom} verse
sa verset her verse
version^{nom} version
ta version your version
vert^{adj} green
la feuill'est vert the leaf is green
vêtement^{nom} garment
portez un vêtement wear a garment
vêtements^{nom.pluriel} clothes
achetez vêtements buy clothes
veuf^{nom} widower
il est un veuf he is a widower
veuvage^{nom} widowhood
un veuvage petit a short widowhood
veuve^{nom} widow
ell'est un veuve she is a widow
viande^{nom} meat
chèvre viande goat meat
vibrer^{act} vibrate
tu vibres you vibrate
vice^{nom} vice
ta vice your vice
victoire^{nom} victory
ta victoire your victory
vidanger^{act} drain
elle vidange she drains
vide^{adj} empty
seau vide empty bucket
vidéo^{nom} video
regarder la vidéo watch the video
vie^{nom.feminin} life
ta vie habites bien your life live well
vieil homme^{nom} old man
sa vieil homme her old man
vieille dame^{nom} old lady
ma vieille dame my old lady
vieux^{adj} old
casserole vieux old pan

village^{nom} village
je visiterai la village I will visit the village
ville^{nom} town

ville^{nom} city
ma ville my city
ville natale^{nom} hometown
ma ville natale my hometown
vingt^{adj} twenty
vingt twenty
vingtième^{adj.masculin} twentieth
le livre vingtième the twentieth book
violet^{adj} violet
la journal est violet the paper is violet
visage^{nom.masculin} face
regardez à mon visage look at my face
visiter^{act} visit
je visite I visit
vitalité^{nom} vitality
sa vitalité her vitality
vivant^{adj.masculin} living
dieu vivant living god
vodka^{nom} vodka

voie^{nom} way
la voie the way
voir^{act} see
tu vois you see
voisin^{nom} neighbour
ma voisin my neighbour
voiture^{nom} car
conduisez un voiture drive a car
voix^{nom} voice
adoucissez ta voix soften your voice
voler^{act} fly
elle vole she flies
voler^{act} steal
volez et détruisez steal and destroy
voleur^{nom} thief
sa voleur her thief
volonté^{nom} will
God's volonté God's will
volume^{nom} volume
ta volume your volume
vomi^{nom} vomit
nettoyer la vomi clean the vomit
vote^{nom} voting
sa vote her voting

voter[act] vote
tu votes you vote
votre[pos] your
tu et tu, votre maison you and you, your house
vouloir[act] want
je voulois le livre I want the book
vous[pro] you
vous mangez la nourriture you eat the food
vous[pro] you
nous saluons vous we greet you
voyage[nom] journey
un voyage longue a long journey
voyage[nom] trip
voyage de Inde trip of India
voyager[nom] exploration
ell'aime voyager she loves exploration
voyager[act] travel
nous voyageons we travel
voyageur[nom] traveller
ma voyageur my traveller
voyant[adj] gaudy
collier voyant gaudy necklace
vrai[adj] true
l'histoire est vrai the story is true
vraiment[adv] truly
vraiment truly
Wolof[nom] Wolof
ta Wolof your Wolof
xylophone[nom.masculin] xylophone
mon xylophone my xylophone
y[adv] there
ell'ira y she will go there
y[pho] y
y y
Yoruba[nom] Yoruba
sa Yoruba her Yoruba
ytterbium[sci] ytterbium
ytterbium est un ytterbium ytterbium is a ytterbium
Zambie[nom.masculin] Zambia
mon Zambie my Zambia
zèbre[nom] zebra
sa zèbre her zebra
zéro[adj] zero
zéro et un zero and one
Zoulou[nom] Zulu
ta Zoulou your Zulu

English-Français

’ a b c d e f g h i j k l m n o p q r s t u v w x y z

a^{det} un
a man, a woman and a child un homme, un femme et un enfant
abdomen^{nom} abdomen
her abdomen sa abdomen
abomination^{nom} abomination
it is an abomination il est une abomination
aborigine^{nom} aborigène
he is an aborigine il est un aborigène
about^{pre} de
about you de toi
abroad^{nom} à l'étranger
my abroad ma à l'étranger
accept^{act} accepter
we accept the gift nous acceptons le cadeau
acceptance^{nom} acceptation
love, acceptance and forgiveness amour, acceptation et pardon
access^{nom} accès
your access ta accès
accident^{nom} accident
car accident voiture accident
account^{nom} compte
bank account banque compte
accountability^{nom} responsabilité
responsibility and accountability responsabilité et responsabilité
accounts^{nom} comptes
her accounts sa comptes
accuse^{act} accuser
I accuse je accuse
acid^{nom.-es plural} acide
"HCl" is an acid "HCl" est un acide
acidic^{adj} acide
acidic water eau acide
act^{nom} acte
act acte
action^{nom} action
my action ma action
activity^{nom} activité
her activity sa activité
actor^{nom.-es plural} acteur
he is an actor il est un acteur
actress^{nom.y->ies plural} actrice
she is an actress ell'est une actrice
ad^{nom} publicité
her ad sa publicité

adapt^{act} changer
time adapts everything temps change tout
add^{act} ajouter
add sugar ajoutez sucre
addition^{nom} addition
her addition sa addition
address^{nom} adresse
your address ta adresse
adjective^{nom} adjectif
the noun has an adjective le nom a un adjectif
adjust^{act} ajuster
she adjusts ell'ajuste
administration^{nom} administration
her administration brings advancement sa administration apporte progrès
admire^{act} admirer
you admire tu admires
adopt^{act} adopter
she adopts ell'adopte
adoption^{nom} adoption
my adoption ma adoption
adulation^{nom} adulation
she deserves adulation elle mérite adulation
adultery^{nom} adultère
adultery and divorce adultère et divorce
advance^{adj} avance
it is advance il est avance
advancement^{nom} progrès
I see advancement je voyez progrès
advantage^{nom} avantage
your advantage ta avantage
adverb^{nom} adverbe
the verb has an adverb le verbe a un adverbe
advice^{nom} conseils
a pastor has advice un prêtre a conseils
aeroplane^{nom} avion
her aeroplane sa avion
Afar^{nom} au loin
he records Afar il écri au loin
affect^{nom} affecter
her affect son affecter
Africa^{nom} Afrique
your Africa ta Afrique
African^{nom} Africain
your African ta Africain
Afrikaans^{nom.-es plural} Afrikaans
she records Afrikaans ell'écri Afrikaans

afternoon^{nom} après-midi
the afternoon is hot l'après-midi est chaud
again^{adv} encore
see voyez
age^{act} grandir
you age tu grandis
age^{nom} âge
your age ta âge
age group^{nom} groupe d'âge
my age group ma groupe d'âge
aggression^{nom} agression
her aggression sa agression
agree^{act} être d'accord
he agrees il est d'accord
ah^{exc} ah
ah yes! ah yes!
aim^{nom} but
the aim of life le but de vie
air^{nom} air
the air is l'air est
airport^{nom} aeroport
her airport son aeroport
Akan^{nom} Akan
Akan is a language Akan est un langue
alcohol^{nom} alcool
he drinks alcohol il boi alcool
alert^{act} alerter
alert them alertez them
Algeria^{nom} Algérie
my Algeria ma Algérie
all^{pro} tout
all are black tout sont noir
all^{det} tout
all things tout des choses
all^{adj} tout
this is all cet est tout
alligator pepper^{nom} poivre d'alligator
her alligator pepper sa poivre d'alligator
allow^{act} permettre
allow them permettsez them
almighty^{adj} tout-puissant
God is almighty Dieu est tout-puissant
Almighty^{nom} Tout-puissant
her Almighty sa Tout-puissant
almost^{adv} presque
almost here presque ici
always^{adv} toujours
he is il est

amazing^{adj} incroyable
the story is amazing l'histoire est incroyable
amen^{exc} amen
hallelujah and amen alléluia et amen
America^{nom} Amérique
my America mon Amérique
American^{nom} Américain
her American son Américain
Amharic^{nom.-es plural} Amharique
her Amharic son Amharique
among^{pre} parmi
among people among gens
amount^{nom} montant
an amount of money un montant de argent
amusing^{adj} amusant
it is amusing il est amusant
ancestor^{nom} ancêtre
my ancestor ma ancêtre
anchor^{nom} ancre
anchor of a ship ancre de un navire
ancient^{adj} ancien
ancient house maison ancien
and^{cjn} et
Kofi and Ama Kofi et Ama
angle^{nom} angle
her angle sa angle
animal^{nom} animal
a dog is an animal un chien est un animal
ankle^{nom} cheville
her ankle sa cheville
announce^{act} annoncer
announce annoncer
announcement^{nom} annonce
read the announcement lisez l'annonce
annoy^{act} gener
she annoys elle gene
annoying^{adj} ennuyeux
it is annoying il est ennuyeux
annul^{act} annuler
annul a marriage annulez un mariage
anoint^{act} oindre
she anoint my head ell'oindsez ma tête
answer^{act} répondre
we answer nous répondsons
answer^{nom} réponse
my answer ma réponse
ant^{nom} fourmi
a red ant un fourmi rouge

antelope^{nom} antilope
a lion likes antelope meat un lion aime antilope viande
anthill^{nom} fourmilière
a tall anthill un fourmilière grand
antiquity^{nom} antiquité
your antiquity ta antiquité
ants^{nom} fourmis

anvil^{nom} enclume
hammer and anvil marteau et enclume
any^{adj} tout
any book livre tout
apathy^{nom} apathie
apathy kill good apathie tuez bon
apparition^{nom} apparition
your apparition ta apparition
appellation^{nom} appellation
her appellation sa appellation
apple^{nom} pomme
eat the apple mangez la pomme
approach^{act} approcher
I approach je approche
apricot^{nom} abricot
your apricot ton abricot
area^{nom} quartier
her area sa quartier
argue^{act} se disputer
we argue every day nous se disputer jour chaque
argument^{nom} argument
my argument ma argument
arise^{act} augmenter
we arise nous augmentons
arm^{nom} bras
your arm ta bras
armpit^{nom} aisselle
her armpit sa aisselle
arrange^{act} organiser

arrive^{act} arriver
she arrives ell'arrive
arrogance^{nom} arrogance
arrogance is bad arrogance est mauvais
arrogant^{adj} arrogant
arrogant man homme arrogant
arrow^{nom} flèche
bow and arrow arc et flèche

artery^{nom} artère
a large artery un artère grand
artist^{nom.-es plural} artiste
she is an artist ell'est un artiste
as^{adv} comme

ash^{nom} cendre
salt and ash sel et cendre
Asia^{nom} Asie
my Asia mon Asie
ask^{act} demander
to ask Kofi demander Kofi
aspiration^{nom} aspiration
good aspiration aspiration bon
assessment^{nom} test
the assessment is difficult la test est difficile
assistance^{nom} assistance
he needs your assistance il a besoin de ton assistance
assistant^{nom} assistant
my assistant ma assistant
association^{nom} association
your association ta association
at^{pre} à
meet me rencontrez moi
Atlantic^{adj} atlantique
Atlantic Ocean Océan Atlantique
attach^{act} attacher
attach to wall attachez à mur
attire^{nom} tenue
your attire is beautiful ta tenue est belle
August^{nom} Août
August is a month Août est un mois
aunt^{nom} tante
our aunt notre tante
Australia^{nom} Australie
we love Australia nous aimons Australie
author^{nom} écrivain
I am an author je suis un écrivain
authority^{nom} puissance
strength and authority force et puissance
Autumn^{nom} automne
your Autumn ton automne
avoid^{act} éviter
avoid evil éviter mal
awaken^{act} éveiller
we awaken nous éveillons

award^{nom} prix
your award ta prix
awesome^{adj} génial
awesome god dieu génial
aye^{exc} oui
Aye! Silence! Aye! Silence!
azonto^{nom} azonto
my azonto ma azonto
baboon^{nom} babouin
your baboon ta babouin
baby^{nom.y->ies plural} bébé
I have a baby j'ai un bébé
back^{nom} arrière
the back of the door l'arrière de la porte
bad^{adj} mauvais
a bad thing un chose mauvais
bag^{nom} sac
you want the bag tu voulois la sac
bake^{act} cuire
bake bread cuisez pain
ball^{nom} balle
play ball jeu balle
balloon^{nom} ballon
her balloon sa ballon
Bambara^{nom} Bambara
Bambara language Bambara langue
banana^{nom} banane
the monkey likes the banana le singe aime la banane
bank^{nom} banque
my money is at the bank ma argent est à la banque

baptise^{act} baptiser
baptise John baptisez John
baptism^{nom} baptême
repentance and baptism repentance et baptême
bargain^{act} négocier
we bargain nous négocions
bark^{act} aboyer
a dog barks un chien aboye
bark^{nom} écorce
bark of a tree écorce de un arbre
barrel^{nom} baril
my barrel ma baril
barren^{adj} stérile
barren woman femme stérile
basic^{adj} simple
it is basic il est simple

basil^{nom} basilic
a basil leaf un basilic feuille
basin^{nom} bassin
my basin ma bassin
basket^{nom} panier
he buys a basket il achete un panier
basketball^{nom} basketball
she plays basketball elle joue basketball
bat^{nom} chauve souris
my bat ma chauve souris
bath^{nom} bain
clean the bath nettoyer le bain
bathe^{act} baigner
I bathe every day je baigne jour chaque
bathroom^{nom} salle de bain
go to the bathroom allez à la salle de bain
battle^{nom} bataille
her battle sa bataille
Baule^{nom} baoulé
I will learn Baule je apprendras baoulé
be^{act} être
you are an important person tu es un personne important
be jealous^{act} être jaloux
she is jealous ell'est jaloux
beach^{nom} plage
beach sand plage sable
bead^{nom} perle
her bead son perle
beaker^{nom} gobelet
her beaker son gobelet
bean^{nom} haricot
rice and beans riz et haricots
bear^{nom} ours
Sisi Kisi is a bear Sisi Kisi est un ours
beard^{nom} barbe
long beard barbe longue
beat^{act} battre
beat someone battsez someone
beautiful^{adj} belle
you are beautiful tu es belle
beauty^{nom} beauté
beauty and love beauté et amour
because^{cjn} parce que
she dances because she likes dancing elle danse parce que ell'aime dans
become^{act} devenir
to become rich devenir riche

bed^{nom} lit
sleep the bed dormez le lit
bedbug^{nom} punaise de lit
your bedbug ta punaise de lit
bedroom^{nom} chambre
your bedroom ta chambre
bedstead^{nom} châlit
my bedstead mon châlit
bee^{nom} abeille
a bee makes honey un abeille fait miel
beef^{nom} bœuf
we eat beef nous mangeons bœuf
beer^{nom} bière
we drink beer nous boisons bière
beetle^{nom.-es plural} scarabée
a red beetle un scarabée rouge
before^{pre} avant
eat mangez
beg^{act} mendier
I beg je mendie
begin^{act} commencer
you begin tu commences
beginner^{nom.-es plural} débutant
he is a beginner il est un débutant
behaviour^{nom} comportement
normal behaviour comportement normal
being^{nom} être
human being humain être
belch^{act} roter
I belch je rote
believe^{act} croire
she believes the child elle croi l'enfant
bell^{nom} cloche
school bell école cloche
belly^{nom} estomac
big belly estomac grand
belly button^{nom} nombril
my belly button mon nombril
beloved^{nom} bien-aimé
your beloved ton bien-aimé
belt^{nom} ceinture
black belt ceinture noir
bench^{nom} banc
a white bench un banc blanc
bend^{act} plier
bend it pliez il
Benin^{nom} Bénin
my Benin ma Bénin

betray^{act} trahir
you betray tu trahis
better^{adj} mieux
it is better il est mieux
better^{adv} mieux
he sings better il chante mieux
bible^{nom} bible
the bible and the koran la bibl'et la Coran
bicycle^{nom} vélo
new bicycle vélo nouveau
big^{adj} grand
a mountain is big un montagne est grand
bile^{nom} bile
green bile bile vert
bill^{nom} facture
her bill sa facture
billion^{adj} milliard
a billion un milliard
billy^{adj} mâle
a billy child un enfant mâle
biology^{nom} biologie
her biology sa biologie
bird^{nom} oiseau
a bird flies un oiseau vole
birth^{act} donner naissance
we birth nous donnons naissance
bishop^{nom} évêque
she is a bishop ell'est un évêque
bite^{act} mordre
the dog bites a stick le chien mord un bâton
bitter^{adj} amer
the drug is bitter la médecine est amer
black^{adj} noir
black cloth chiffon noir
blanket^{nom} couverture
wet blanket couverture mouillé
bleed^{act} saigner
I bleed je saigne
bleeding^{nom} hémorragie
bleeding is bad hémorragie est mauvais
bless^{act} bénir
bless me bénissez me
blessing^{nom} bénédiction
the blessing of God la bénédiction de Dieu
block^{act} bloquer
you block tu bloques
blog^{nom} Blog
food blog nourriture Blog

blood^{nom} sang
 water and blood eau et sang
blow^{act} souffler
 you blow air tu souffles air
blow^{nom} coup
 your blow ta coup
blowfly^{nom} mouche à viande
 blowfly are annoying mouche à viande êtes ennuyeux

blue^{adj} bleu
 the dress is blue la robe est bleu
blueprint^{nom} plan
 a pot and a blueprint un pot et un plan
boat^{nom} bateau
 red boat bateau rouge
bodice^{nom} corsage
 she wears a bodice elle porte un corsage
body^{nom} corps
 her body son corps
boil^{act} bouillir
 he boils il bouillit
bomb^{nom} bombe
 the bomb explode la bombe explosez
bone^{nom} os
 my hand has bones ma main a oss
bonus^{nom} bonus
 I want a bonus je voulois un bonus
book^{nom} livre
 this book ce livre
boring^{adj} ennuyeuse
 the story is boring l'histoire est ennuyeuse
borrow^{act} emprunter
 borrow money empruntez argent
boss^{nom} patron
 my boss mon patron
bother^{act} déranger
 the dog bothers le chien dérange
bother^{nom} déranger
 your bother ton déranger
bottle^{nom} bouteille
 my bottle ma bouteille
bow^{nom} arc
 bow and arrow arc et flèche
bow-legged^{adj} aux jambes arquées
 bow-legged man homme aux jambes arquées
bowl^{nom} bol
 a red bowl un bol rouge

box^{nom} boîte
 a big box un boîte grand
boxing^{nom} boxe
 boxing is a sport boxe est un sport
boy^{nom} garçon
 the boy is le garçon est
boyfriend^{nom} copain
 my boyfriend mon copain
bracket^{nom.-es plural} support
 she records a bracket ell'écri un support
brain^{nom} cerveau
 the brain and the mind la cerveau et l'esprit
brake^{act} freiner
 I brake je freine
brake^{nom} frein
 brake of a car frein de un voiture
branch^{act} brancher
 she branchs elle branche
branch^{nom} branche
 family branch famille branche
brave^{adj} courageux
 brave man homme courageux
bread^{nom} pain
 we will eat bread nous mangerons pain
breadth^{nom} largeur
 breadth and width largeur et largeur
break^{act} casser
 break the stick cassez la bâton
breakfast^{nom} petit déjeuner
 my breakfast mon petit déjeuner
breast^{nom} poitrine
 breast of man poitrine de homme
breastmilk^{nom} lait maternel
 drink the breastmilk boisez la lait maternel
breath^{nom} souffle
 a breath of air un souffle de air
breathe^{act} respirer
 you breathe tu respires
bribe^{nom} pot-de-vin
 he wants a bribe il vouloit un pot-de-vin
brick^{nom} brique
 your brick ta brique
bride^{nom} jeune mariée
 bride jeune mariée
bridegroom^{nom} marié
 her bridegroom sa marié
bridge^{nom} pont
 we will build a bridge nous construirons un pont

brief^{adj} bref
it is brief il est bref
bright^{adj} brillant
the room is bright la chambre est brillant
bring^{act} apporter
he will bring a book il apportera un livre
brook^{nom} ruisseau
your brook ta ruisseau
broom^{nom} balai
broom and dustpan balai et balayette
brother^{nom} frère
her brother son frère
brown^{adj} brun
the bird is brown l'oiseau est brun
brush^{nom} brosse
a black brush un brosse noir
bucket^{nom} seau
the bucket is red le seau est rouge
bud^{nom} bourgeon
flower bud fleur bourgeon
budget^{nom} budget
her budget sa budget
build^{act} construire
we build a house nous construisons un maison
building^{nom.-es plural} bâtiment
the building is new le bâtiment est nouveau
bullet^{nom} balle
my bullet ma balle
bully^{nom} brute
he is a bully il est un brute
bungalow^{nom} bungalow
my bungalow mon bungalow
burden^{nom} fardeau
my burden ma fardeau
burglary^{nom} cambriolage
burglary is cambriolage est
Burkina Faso^{nom} Burkina Faso
my Burkina Faso ma Burkina Faso
burn^{act} brûler
burn papers brûlez papers
bury^{act} enterrer
I bury je enterre
bus^{nom} bus
the bus is red le bus est rouge
bush^{nom} brousse

business^{nom} affaires
my business ma affaires

busy^{adj} occupé
it is busy il est occupé
but^{cjn} mais
she eats food but he drinks water elle mange nourriture mais il boi eau
butter^{nom} beurre
bread and butter pain et beurre
butterfly^{nom} papillon
a butterfly is beautiful un papillon est belle
buttocks^{nom} fesses
big buttocks fesses grand
button^{nom} bouton
press the button appuyer le bouton
buy^{act} acheter
they will buy a car elles acheteront un voiture
buyer^{nom} acheteur
my buyer ma acheteur
by any chance^{adv} par hasard
have you avez tu
cake^{nom} gâteau
cake and wine gâteau et du vin
calendar^{nom} calendrier
a new calendar un calendrier nouveau
California^{nom} Californie
the state of California l'état de Californie
call^{act} appeler
to call the boy appeler le garçon
camel^{nom} chameau
your camel is old ta chameau est vieux
camera^{nom} appareil photographique
lens of a camera lentille de un appareil photographique

Cameroon^{nom} Cameroun
your Cameroon ta Cameroun
camp^{nom} camp
go to the camp allez à la camp
can^{act} pouvoir
I can
Canada^{nom} Canada
your Canada ton Canada
cancel^{act} annuler
cancel the meeting annulez la réunion
cancer^{nom} cancer
cancer is a disease cancer est un maladie
cane^{nom} canne
bring the cane apportez la canne
cannon^{nom} canon
shoot the cannon tirez la canon

canvas^{nom} toile
 a large canvas un toile grand
capable^{adj} capable
 a capable woman un femme capable
capital^{nom} capitale
 the capital of Ghana la capitale de Ghana
captain^{nom} capitaine
 she is a captain ell'est un capitaine
car^{nom} voiture
 drive a car conduisez un voiture
card^{nom} carte
 a white card un carte blanc
care^{act} se soucier
 you care tu se soucier
carefulness^{nom} soin
 my carefulness mon soin
caress^{act} caresser
 her hand caress it sa main caressez il
Caribbean^{nom} Caraïbes
 her Caribbean sa Caraïbes
carpenter^{nom} charpentier
 he needs a carpenter il a besoin de un charpentier

carpentry^{nom} menuiserie
 she knows carpentry elle connaît menuiserie
carpet^{nom} tapis
 new carpet tapis nouveau
carrot^{nom} carotte
 my carrot ma carotte
carry^{act} porter
 you carry the book tu portes le livre
carton^{nom} carton
 carton of milk carton de lait
cartoon^{nom} dessin animé
 your cartoon ton dessin animé
cash^{nom} argent
 I have cash je avez argent
cassava^{nom} manioc
 plantain and cassava plantain et manioc
cast^{nom} cast
 cast of a film cast de un film
cat^{nom} chat
 the cat has a tail le chat a un queue
catarrh^{nom} catarrhe
 I have catarrh je avez catarrhe
catch^{act} attraper
 I catch the ball je attrape le balle

catechumen chrétien nouveau

category^{nom} catégorie
 your category ta catégorie
caterpillar^{nom} chenille
 a caterpillar becomes a butterfly un chenille devenit un papillon
cease^{act} arrêter
 cease the noise arrêter la bruit
cedi^{nom} cedi
 hundred pesewa make one cedi pesewa cent faites cedi un
cell^{nom} cellule
 the skin has cells la peau a cellules
cement^{nom} ciment
 her cement sa ciment
centre^{nom} milieu
 are in the centre êtes dans la milieu
century^{nom} siècle
 this century ce siècle
certificate^{nom} certificat
 your certificate ta certificat
chain^{nom} chaîne
 my chain ma chaîne
chair^{nom} chaise
 they bring the chair elles apportent la chaise
chairman^{nom} président
 her chairman son président
chairwoman^{nom} présidente
 my chairwoman ma présidente
chalk^{nom} craie
 white chalk craie blanc
challenge^{nom} défi
 a good challenge un défi bon
chameleon^{nom} caméléon
 I see the chameleon je voyez la caméléon
change^{nom} change
 your change ta change
chaotic^{adj} chaotique
 the place is chaotic la place est chaotique
chapter^{nom} chapitre
 chapter chapitre
character^{nom} caractère
 her character sa caractère
charcoal^{nom} charbon de bois
 sack of charcoal sac de charbon de bois
charge^{sci} charge
 an electron has charge un électron a charge

chase^{act} chasser
the dog chases le chien chasse
cheap^{adj} pas cher
the bread is cheap le pain est pas cher
cheat^{act} tricher
she cheats elle triche
cheek^{nom} joue
my cheek ma joue
cheese^{nom} fromage
blue cheese fromage bleu
chef^{nom} chef
a good chef un chef bon
chemistry^{nom} chimie
we learn chemistry nous apprendsons chimie
cheque^{nom} chèque
record a cheque écrisez un chèque
chest^{nom} poitrine
chest hair poitrine cheveux
chew^{act} mâcher
we chew nous mâchons
Chewa^{nom} Chewa
her Chewa sa Chewa
chicken^{nom} poulet
chicken meat poulet viande
chickenpox^{nom} varicelle
chickenpox is a disease varicell'est un maladie
chief^{nom} chef
she is a chief ell'est un chef
chieftain^{nom} chef de clan
my chieftain mon chef de clan
child^{nom} enfant
my child ma enfant
childbirth^{nom} accouchement
a childbirth brings joy un accouchement apporte joie
childhood^{nom} enfance
my childhood ma enfance
chimpanzee^{nom} chimpanzé
I see a chimpanzee je voyez un chimpanzé
chin^{nom} menton
you hold your chin tu tenis ton menton
chocolate^{nom} chocolat
the chocolate has le chocolat a
choose^{act} choisir
choose good choisir bien
Christ^{nom} Christ
my Christ mon Christ

Christian^{nom} chrétien
your Christian ta chrétien
Christianity^{nom} Christianisme
her Christianity sa Christianisme
Christmas^{nom} noël
my family love Christmas ma famill'aiment noël
church^{nom} église
church and country église et pays
cigarette^{nom} cigarette
my cigarette ma cigarette
cilantro^{nom} coriandre
cilantro is a plant coriandre est un plante
cinema^{nom} cinéma
we like the cinema nous aimons la cinéma
circle^{nom} cercle
circle and line cercl'et ligne
circumstance^{nom} circonstance
her circumstance sa circonstance
citizen^{nom} citoyen
I am a citizen of earth je suis un citoyen de terre
city^{nom} ville
my city ma ville
civil war^{nom} guerre civile
my civil war ma guerre civile
civilized^{adj} civilisé
a civilized world un monde civilisé
claim^{act} prétendre
you claim tu prétends
clap^{act} applaudir
you clap tu applaudis
clarion^{adj} clairon
a clarion warning un avertissement clairon
class^{nom} étage
he is in class il est dans étage
classroom^{nom.-es plural} salle de cours
the classroom is clean la salle de cours est nettoyer

clay^{nom} argile
clay vase argile vase
clean^{adj} nettoyer
the house is clean la maison est nettoyer
clear^{adj} clair
clear sky ciel clair
clearly^{adv} clairement
you see it tu voyez il
clever^{adj} intelligent
it is clever il est intelligent

click[act] cliquer
click here cliquez ici
climb[act] gravir
he climbs the tree il gravit l'arbre
clinic[nom] hôpital
go to a clinic allez à un hôpital
clock[nom] horloge
your clock ta horloge
close[act] fermer
close the door fermer la porte
cloth[nom] chiffon
wear cloth portez chiffon
clothes[nom] vêtements
buy clothes achetez vêtements
cloud[nom] nuage
a white cloud un nuage blanc
cloudy[adj] nuageux
a cloudy day un jour nuageux
clove[nom] clou de girofle
add a clove ajoutez un clou de girofle
coach[nom] entraîneur
my coach ma entraîneur
coaltar[nom] coaltar
hot coaltar coaltar chaud
coast[nom] côte
gold coast or côte
coat[nom] manteau
my coat mon manteau
cobra[nom] cobra
black cobra cobra noir
cockerel[nom] coquelet
a cockerel is un coquelet est
cockroach[nom] cafard
I see a cockroach je voyez un cafard
cocoa[nom] cacao
cocoa tree cacao arbre
coconut[nom] noix de coco
my coconut ma noix de coco
cocoyam[nom] taro
I like cocoyam j'aimez taro
cocoyam leaves[nom] taro feuilles
your cocoyam leaves tes taro feuilles
code[nom] code
your code ta code
coffee[nom] café
she drink coffee elle boisez café
coin[nom] pièce de monnaie
her coin sa pièce de monnaie

cold[adj] du froid
the water is cold l'eau est du froid
collander[nom] passoire
use the collander utilisez la passoire
collect[act] ramasser
I collect je ramasse
color[nom] couleur
I like your color j'aime ta couleur
colour[act] colorier
colour and learn colorier et apprendre
comb[act] peigne
I comb my hair je peigne mes cheveux
comb[nom] peigne
use a comb utilisez un peigne
come[act] venir
come here! venissez here!
comfort[nom] confort
your comfort ta confort
comfortable[adj] comfortable
the sofa is comfortable le canapé est comfortable
command[act] commander
you command tu commandes
command[nom] commande
her command sa commande
committee[nom] comité
I will join the committee je se raccorder le comité

community[nom] communauté
a community of people un communauté de gens
company[nom] entreprise
a small company un entreprise petit
compassion[nom] la compassion
she has compassion ell'a la compassion
compensation[nom] rémunération
your compensation ta rémunération
comprehension[nom] compréhension
comprehension is important compréhension est important
computer[nom] ordinateur
computer keyboard ordinateur clavier
computing[nom] informatique
her computing sa informatique
conference[nom] conférence
your conference ta conférence
confidence[nom] confiance
I have confidence je avez confiance
Congo[nom] Congo
my Congo ma Congo

congratulations^{nom} félicitations
congratulations and well done félicitations et bien fait
conjunction^{nom.-es plural} conjonction

conjunctivitis^{nom} conjonctivite
conjunctivitis is a disease conjonctivite est un maladie
connection^{nom.-es plural} connexion
this chain has one connection ce chaîne a un connexion
conscience^{nom} conscience
your conscience ta conscience
consequence^{nom} conséquence
your consequence ta conséquence
consist^{act} constituer
I consist je constitue
consolation^{nom} consolation
love and consolation amour et consolation
contempt^{nom} mépris
your contempt ta mépris
continent^{nom} continent
African continent African continent
continue^{act} continuer
continue the work continuez le travail
cook^{act} cuire
to cook the food cuire la nourriture
cool^{act} refroidir
we cool nous refroidissons
cool^{adj} cool
a cool beer un bière cool
coop^{nom} poulailler
she builds a coop elle construi un poulailler
corn^{nom} maïs
corn and groundnut maïs et arachide
corners^{nom} coins
your corners ta coins
corpse^{nom} cadavre
the corpse is la cadavre est
cost^{nom} coût
your cost ta coût
Cote d'Ivoire^{nom} Côte d'Ivoire
her Cote d'Ivoire sa Côte d'Ivoire
cottage un maison petit

cotton^{nom} coton
cotton is white coton est blanc

cough^{act} tousser
the baby coughs la bébé tousse
cough^{nom} toux
he has a cough il a un toux
councillor^{nom} conseiller
she is a councillor ell'est un conseiller
count^{act} compter
we count the money nous comptons l'argent
country^{nom} pays
your country ta pays
courage^{nom} courage
she has courage ell'a courage
courageous^{adj} courageux
it is courageous il est courageux
courier^{nom} messager
the courier arrive la messager arrivez
court^{nom} tribunal
the court of justice la tribunal de justice
cousin^{nom.-es plural} cousin
my cousin mon cousin
covenant^{nom} alliance
my covenant ma alliance
cover^{act} couvrir
cover it couvrissez il
covetuousness^{nom} covetuousness
her covetuousness sa covetuousness
cow^{nom} vache
a cow eats grass un vache mange herbe
crab^{nom} crabe
crab likes water crabe aime eau
crawl^{act} ramper
the baby crawls la bébé rampe
create^{act} créer
something create new quelque chose créez nouveau
creation^{nom} création
all creation tout création
creator^{nom} créateur
creator god créateur dieu
crocodile^{nom} crocodile
a crocodile likes water un crocodil'aime eau
cross^{act} traverser
you cross tu traverses
cross^{nom} croix
the cross of Christ la croix de Christ
crow^{nom} corbeau
a black crow un corbeau noir

crowd^{nom} foule
noisy crowd noisy foule
crown^{nom} couronne
a crown of gold un couronne de or
cry^{act} pleurer
she cries elle pleure
crystal^{nom} cristal
a beautiful cristal un cristal belle
cube^{nom} cube
a cube of sugar un cube de sucre
culture^{nom} culture
the culture of my school la culture de mon école
cunning^{adj} rusé
a cunning woman un femme rusé
cup^{nom} tasse
tea cup thé tasse
curse^{nom} malédiction
a prayer and a curse un prière et un malédiction
curtain^{nom} rideau
the window needs a curtain la fenêtre a besoin de
un rideau
custom^{nom} coutume
love is a good custom amour est un coutume bon
customer^{nom} client
a good customer un client bon
cut^{act} couper
cut the paper couper la journal
cutlass^{nom} coutelas
my cutlass ma coutelas
cymbal^{nom} cymbale
play the cymbal jouez la cymbale
dad^{nom} père
your dad ton père
daily^{adv} quotidiennement
he comes il venit
dance^{act} danser
to dance well danser bien
danger^{nom} danger
he is in danger il est dans danger
dangerous^{adj} dangereux
a dangerous game un jeu dangereux
dark^{adj} sombre
the night is dark la nuit est sombre
darkness^{nom} obscurité
night brings darkness nuit apporte obscurité
darling^{nom} bien-aimé
my darling has ma bien-aimé a

date^{nom} date
I know the date je connaîts la date
daughter^{nom} fille
my daughter ma fille
dawn^{nom} aube
a new dawn un aube nouveau
day^{nom} jour
day and night jour et nuit
daybreak^{nom} aube
daybreak and nightfall aube et tombée de la nuit
dead^{adj} mort
a dead tree un arbre mort
death^{nom} décès
place of death place de décès
debate^{nom} débat
the debate is la débat est
debt^{nom} dette
your debt ta dette
decade^{nom} décennie
this decade ce décennie
decagon^{nom} décagone
a decagon has ten un décagone a dix
decay^{nom.y->ies plural} décomposition
decay is bad décomposition est mauvais
deceive^{act} duper
we deceive nous dupons
December^{nom} Décembre
Sunday. December 25, 1960 Dimanche. Décembre
25, 1960
deception^{nom} tromperie
deception and discord tromperie et discorde
decrease^{act} réduire
decrease it réduisez il
deduct^{act} déduire
deduct one déduisez un
deep^{adj} profond
a deep hole un trou profond
deer^{nom} cerf
a lion likes deers un lion aime cerfs
defeat^{nom} défaite
my defeat ma défaite
defecate^{act} déféquer
we defecate nous déféquons
defile^{act} souiller
she defiles elle souille
deflate^{act} dégonfler
they deflate elles dégonflent

delay[act] retarder
he delays il retarde
delightful[adj] délicieux
delightful work travail délicieux
deliver[act] distribuer
deliver money distribuez argent
delivery[nom] livraison
the delivery has la livraison a
demand[nom] demande
demand and supply demande et offre
deny[act] nier
we deny nous nions
deplete[act] épuiser
we deplete nous épuisons
desert[nom] désert
her desert sa désert
deserve[act] mériter
I deserve je mérite
desirable[adj] souhaitable
it is desirable il est souhaitable
desire[nom] désir
your desire ta désir
destroy[act.-es plural] détruire
they destroy the book elles détruisent le livre
determination[nom] détermination
her determination sa détermination
development[nom] développement
my development ma développement
devil[nom] diable
her devil sa diable
dew[nom] rosée
morning dew matin rosée
diamond[nom] diamant
a white diamond un diamant blanc
diarrhoea[nom] la diarrhée
diarrhoea and fever la diarrhée et fièvre
dictionary[nom] dictionnaire
image dictionary image dictionnaire
die[act] mourir
everyone will die tout le monde mouriront
different[adj] différent
we are different nous sommes différent
difficult[adj] difficile
the work is difficult le travail est difficile
dig[act] creuser
she digs elle creuse
dine[act] dîner
you dine tu dînes

dirt[nom] saleté
dirt and disease saleté et maladie
dirty[adj] sale
dirty dress robe sale
disappear[act] disparaître
the dog disappears le chien disparaît
disappoint[act] décevoir
I disappoint je décevois
disappointment[nom] déception
love has disappointment amour a déception
discard[act] jeter
discard the ball jetez le balle
discipline[act] discipliner
discipline your child disciplinez ta enfant
discord[nom] discorde
your discord ta discorde
disease[nom] maladie
heal disease guérissez maladie
disgrace[nom] disgrâce
shame and disgrace honte et disgrâce
disgusting[adj] dégoûtant
the floor is disgusting la sol est dégoûtant
dish[nom] assiette
launder your dish lavez ta assiette
disposition[nom] disposition
your disposition ta disposition
diss[nom] diss
my diss ma diss
distinguished[adj] distingué
the family is distinguished la famill'est distingué

divide[act] diviser
divide the bread divisez le pain
division[nom] division
my division ma division
divorce[nom] divorce
marriage and divorce mariage et divorce
do[act] faire
the dog does le chien fait
doctor[nom] médecin
my doctor is new ma médecin est nouveau
dog[nom] chien
a dog barks un chien aboye
doll[nom] poupée
my doll ma poupée
dollar[nom] dollar
her dollar sa dollar
done[done, dy f a i]

donkey^{nom} âne
 my donkey ma âne
door^{nom} porte
 close the door fermez la porte
doubt^{nom} doute
 she has doubts ell'a doutes
dough^{nom} pâte
 he press the dough il appuyez la pâte
dove^{nom} colombe
 white dove colombe blanc
down^{adv} en bas
 go down allez down
download^{act} télécharger
 download the song télécharger la chanson
downward^{adv} vers le bas

doze^{act} sommeiller
 I doze je sommeille
drain^{act} vidanger
 she drains elle vidange
draw^{act} dessiner
 draw a bird dessinez un oiseau
drawers^{nom} tiroirs
 your drawers ta tiroirs
dream^{act} rêver
 you dream tu rêves
dream^{nom} rêve
 your dream ta rêve
dress^{nom} robe
 blue dress robe bleu
drink^{act} boire
 you drink tu bois
drive^{act} conduire
 drive a car conduisez un voiture
driver^{nom} conducteur
 the driver has la conducteur a
drop^{nom} goutte
 your drop ta goutte
drop^{act} laisser tomber
 to drop the egg laisser tomber le œuf
drown^{act} noyer
 she drowns elle noye
drowsiness^{nom} somnolence
 her drowsiness sa somnolence
drug^{nom} médecine
 bitter drug médecine amer
drum^{nom} tambour
 I hear the drum je entendsez la tambour

drummer^{nom} batteur
 she is a drummer ell'est un batteur
drunkard^{nom} ivrogne
 he is a drunkard il est un ivrogne
drunkenness^{nom} ivresse
 drunkenness and pain ivresse et douleur
dry^{adj} sec
 the land is dry la terre est sec
dry^{act} sécher
 you dry tu séches
dry season^{nom} saison sèche
 your dry season ta saison sèche
duck^{nom} canard
 white duck canard blanc
dumb^{adj} stupide
 it is dumb il est stupide
dung^{nom} bouse
 cow dung vache bouse
duration^{nom} durée
 forty-hour duration forty-hour durée
dust^{nom} poussière
 red dust poussière rouge
dustpan^{nom} balayette
 broom and dustpan balai et balayette
dwarf^{nom} nain
 my dwarf ma nain
dye^{nom} colorant
 black dye colorant noir
each^{adj} chaque
 each thing chose chaque
each and everyone^{pro} chacun
 we love each and everyone nous aimons chacun
ear^{nom} oreille
 ear and nose oreill'et nez
early^{adv} tôt
 come early venissez de bonne heure
early^{adj} de bonne heure
 early morning matin de bonne heure
earpiece^{nom} oreillette
 new earpiece oreillette nouveau
earring^{nom} boucle d'oreille
 he wears earring il porte boucle d'oreille
earth^{nom} terre
 good earth terre bon
earthquake^{nom} tremblement de terre
 the earthquake comes la tremblement de terre venit

east^{nom} est
go east allez est
easy^{adj} facile
the work is easy le travail est facile
eat^{act} manger
I eat je mange
ebola^{nom} ebola
ebola is a disease ebol'est un maladie
economy^{nom} économie
the economy of Africa l'économie de Afrique
education^{nom} éducation
health and education santé et éducation
eel^{nom} anguille
her eel sa anguille
efficiency^{nom.y->ies plural} efficacité
the efficiency of an engine l'efficacité de un moteur
effort^{nom} effort
a good effort un effort bon
egg^{nom} œuf
chicken egg poulet œuf
eight^{adj} huit
eight dogs chiens huits
eight days^{nom} huit jours
your eight days ta huit jours
eight persons^{nom} huit personnes
my eight persons ma huit personnes
eighteen^{adj} dix-huit
eighteen dix-huit
eighteenth^{adj} dix-huitième
the eighteenth cat le chat dix-huitième
eighty^{adj} quatre-vingt
it is eighty il est quatre-vingt
elastic^{adj} élastique
the string is elastic la chaîne est élastique
elder^{adj} aîné
my elder sibling ma enfant de mêmes parents aîné

electric^{adj} électrique
electric light lumière électrique
electricity^{sci} électricité
we want electricity nous vouloissons électricité
electron^{sci} électron
the electric charge of an electron is -1 la charge électrique de un électron est -1
electronic^{adj} électronique
an electronic machine un machine électronique

eleven^{adj} onze
eleven onze
email^{nom} e-mail
print the email imprimez l'e-mail
emotion^{nom.-es plural} sentiment
joy is an emotion joie est un sentiment
emphasis^{exc} accentuation
I are je êtes
employer^{nom.-es plural} employeur
your employer is good ton employeur est bon
empty^{adj} vide
empty bucket seau vide
encourage^{act} encourager
encourage encourager
encouragement^{nom} encouragement
encouragement and joy encouragement et joie
end^{nom} fin
my end ma fin
energy^{sci} énergie
mass and energy masse et énergie
engine^{nom} moteur
a new engine un moteur nouveau
engineer^{nom} ingénieur
an engineer makes a tool un ingénieur fait un outil

England^{nom} Angleterre
your England ton Angleterre
English^{nom} Anglais
we read English nous lisons Anglais
enmity^{nom} inimitié
great enmity inimitié grand
enter^{act} entrer

entertain^{act} divertir
entertain yourself divertissez yourself
entire^{adj} tout
the entire house la maison tout
entry^{nom} entrée
a new entry un entrée nouveau
envy^{nom} envie
gred and envy avidité et envie
Eritrea^{nom} Erythrée
your Eritrea ta Erythrée
espionage^{nom} espionnage
espionage films espionnage films
estimate^{act} estimer
estimate your height estimez ta hauteur

eternal^{adj} éternel
eternal life vie éternel
eternity^{nom} éternité
her eternity sa éternité
Ethiopia^{nom} Ethiopie
her Ethiopia sa Ethiopie
evening^{nom} soir
this evening ce soir
event^{nom} événement
her event son événement
every^{adj} chaque
every house maison chaque
everyone^{pro} tout le monde
everyone will come tout le monde veniront
everything^{pro} tout
everything is new tout est nouveau
everywhere^{pro} partout
everywhere is hot partout est chaud
evil^{nom} mal
which evil is quel mal est
exam^{nom} exam
the exam is easy l'exam est facile
example^{nom} exemple
a good example un exemple bon
except^{cjn} sauf
except god except dieu
excuse me^{exc} excusez moi

executioner^{nom} bourreau
my executioner ma bourreau
expensive^{adj} cher
it is expensive il est cher
experience^{nom} expérience
she has experience ell'a expérience
expertise^{nom} savoir faire
she has expertise ell'a savoir faire
explain^{act} expliquer
I explain je explique
explode^{act} exploser
the bomb explode la bombe explosez
exploration^{nom.-es plural} voyager
she loves exploration ell'aime voyager
extension^{nom} extension
house extension maison extension
exult^{act} exulter
exult exulter
eyeball^{nom} globe oculaire
eye and eyeball œil et globe oculaire

eyebrow^{nom} sourcil
eye and eyebrow œil et sourcil
eyelash^{nom} cil
black eyelash cil noir
fable^{nom} fable
her fable sa fable
fabric^{nom} tissu
her fabric sa tissu
face^{nom} visage
look at my face regardez à mon visage
faith^{nom} foi
faith and peace foi et paix
falcon^{nom} faucon
my falcon mon faucon
fall^{act} tomber
I fall je tombe
falsification^{nom} falsification
her falsification sa falsification
familiar^{adj} familier
a familiar animal un animal familier
fan^{nom} ventilateur
electric fan ventilateur électrique
fare well^{exc} au revoir
fare well, my friend au revoir, ma ami
farm^{nom} ferme
cocoa farm cacao ferme
farmer^{nom} agriculteur
she is a farmer ell'est un agriculteur
fart^{nom} pet
her fart smells sa pet sentit
fast^{adj} rapide
a fast horse un cheval vite
fasting^{nom} jeûne
prayer and fasting prière et jeûne
fat^{adj} graisse
fat graisse
favouritism^{nom} favoritisme
my favouritism ma favoritisme
fear^{nom} peur
fear has peur a
feather^{nom} plume
my feather ma plume
February^{nom} Février
Sunday. February 14, 1960 Dimanche. Février 14, 1960
feel^{act} sentir
he feels her love il sentit sa amour

female^{nom} femelle

my female ma femelle

female^{adj} femelle

a female child un enfant femelle

fence^{nom} clôture

my fence ma clôture

fertile^{adj} fertile

fertile land terre fertile

festival^{nom} festival

her festival sa festival

fetish^{nom} fétiche

this town has a fetish ce vill'a un fétiche

fever^{nom} fièvre

she has a fever ell'a un fièvre

fifteen^{adj} quinze

fifteen quinze

fifteenth^{adj} quinzième

the fifteenth song la chanson quinzième

fifty^{adj} cinquante

fifty cinquante

fight^{act} se battre

she fights elle se battre

file^{nom} fichier

computer file ordinateur fichier

fill^{act} remplir

fill it remplissez it

film^{nom} film

cast of a film cast de un film

filthy^{adj} crasseux

the house is filthy la maison est crasseux

find^{act} trouver

find the word trouvez la mot

finger^{nom} doigt

your finger ton doigt

finish^{act} finir

to finish the work finir le travail

fire^{nom} feu

her fire sa feu

firewood^{nom} bois de chauffage

pickup firewood pickup bois de chauffage

first^{adj} première

the first child l'enfant première

firstborn^{nom} premier-né

my firstborn ma premier-né

fish^{nom.-es plural} poisson

fish is food poisson est nourriture

fisherman^{nom} pêcheur

he is a fisherman il est un pêcheur

fist^{nom} poing

your fist ta poing

five^{adj} cinq

five cinq

five persons^{nom} cinq personnes

my five persons ma cinq personnes

fix^{act} réparer

she will fix the car elle réparera la voiture

flag^{nom} drapeau

yellow flag drapeau jaune

flesh^{nom} chair

flesh and blood chair et sang

flint^{nom} silex

use the flint utilisez la silex

flood^{nom} inondation

Accra flood Accra inondation

floor^{nom} sol

the floor la sol

flour^{nom} farine

corn flour maïs farine

flow^{act} couler

the water flows l'eau coule

flower^{nom} fleur

the flower is white la fleur est blanc

flute^{nom} flûte

my flute ma flûte

fly^{act} voler

she flies elle vole

fly^{nom} mouche

a fly flies un mouche vole

fold^{act} replier

we fold nous replions

foliage^{nom} feuillage

cut the foliage coupez la feuillage

follow^{act} suivre

follow me suitez me

folly^{nom} folie

her folly sa folie

food^{nom} nourriture

to eat food manger nourriture

fool^{nom} imbécile

her fool sa imbécile

foolish^{adj} folle

a foolish story un histoire folle

foot^{nom} le pied

my foot ma le pied

for^{pre} pour

for ourselves for ourselves

forbid[act] interdire
forbid interdire
force[act] force
I force je force
force[nom] force
my force ma force
forehead[nom] front
look at her forehead regardez à sa front
foreigner[nom] étranger

foresee[act] prévoir
we foresee nous prévoissons
forest[nom] forêt
her forest sa forêt
forever[adv] toujours
she live ell'habitez
forget[act] oublier
you forget tu oublies
forgive[act] pardonner
forgive me pardonnez moi
forgiveness[nom] pardon
*love, acceptance and forgiveness amour, accep-
tation et pardon*
fork[nom] fourchette
fork and knife fourchette et couteau
fortress[nom] forteresse
god is my fortress dieu est ma forteresse
forty[adj] quarante
forty quarante
forward[adv] en avant
go forward aller en avant
foundation[nom] fondation
foundation of the house fondation de la maison
four[adj] quatre
it is four il est quatre
four persons personnes quatres

fourteen[adj] quatorze
fourteen quatorze
fourth[adj] quatrième
the fourth girl la fille quatrième
fox[nom] renard
I see a fox je vois un renard
fragrance[nom] parfum
*the fragrance of sheabutter la parfum de beurre
de karité*
framework[nom] cadre
the framework of the house la cadre de la maison

France[nom] France
your France ta France
frankly[adv] franchement
say it disez il
free[adj] gratuit
free food nourriture gratuit
freedom[nom] liberté
freedom and justice liberté et justice
freezing[adj] gelé
the water is freezing l'eau est gelé
French[nom] français
my French ma français
fresh[adj] frais
the water is fresh l'eau est frais
friction[nom] friction
friction come friction venissez
Friday[nom] Vendredi
my Friday ma Vendredi
friend[nom] ami
my friend has a house ma ami a un maison
frighten[act] effrayer
frighten evil people effrayez mal gens
frog[nom] grenouille
a frog likes water un grenouill'aime eau
from[pre] de
go allez
front[nom] avant
the front of the book l'avant du livre
fruit[nom] fruit
we eat fruit nous mangeons fruit
frustration[nom.-es plural] frustration
*some frustration is good quelques frustration est
bon*
fry[act] frire
she fries elle fri
fufu[nom] fufu
eat fufu mangez fufu
Fula[nom] Peul
Fula language Peul langue
fulfil[act] achever
she fulfils the work ell'acheve le travail
full[adj] plein
full bucket seau plein
funeral[nom] enterrement
her funeral sa enterrement
funny[adj] amusant
the story is funny l'histoire est amusant

future^{nom} avenir
my future ma avenir
GaDangme^{nom} GaDangme
my GaDangme ma GaDangme
gallon^{nom} gallon
a gallon of water un gallon de eau
game^{nom} jeu
her game sa jeu
gang^{nom} groupe
her gang sa groupe
gap^{nom} écart
she has a beautiful gap ell'a un écart belle
garage^{nom} garage
car garage voiture garage
garden^{nom} jardin
our garden notre jardin
garment^{nom} vêtement
wear a garment portez un vêtement
gaudy^{adj} voyant
gaudy necklace collier voyant
Gbe^{nom} Gbe
your Gbe ta Gbe
generosity^{nom} générosité
your generosity ta générosité
gentle^{adj} doux
a gentle tongue un langue doux
gently^{adv} doucement

get^{act} prendre
get the book prendsez le livre
get lost^{act} se perdre
I get lost je se perdre
Ghana^{nom} Ghana
we love Ghana nous aimons Ghana
ghost^{nom} fantôme
I see a ghost je voyez un fantôme
giant^{adj} géant
he is a giant man il est un homme géant
giant^{nom} géant
your giant ta géant
gift^{nom} cadeau
good gift cadeau bon
ginger^{nom} gingembre
ginger soup gingembre soupe
ginseng^{nom} ginseng
ginseng is a plant ginseng est un plante
giraffe^{nom} girafe
a giraffe is an animal une girafe est un animal

girl^{nom} fille
tall girl fille grande
give^{act} donner
give the water donnez l'eau
glorify^{act} glorifier
I glorify God je glorifie Dieu
glory^{nom} gloire
glory of humankind gloire de humanité
glutton^{nom} glouton
he is a glutton il est un glouton
go^{act} aller
we go nous allons
goat^{nom} chèvre
a goat and a une chèvre et un
god^{nom} dieu
dependable god dieu fiable
gold^{nom} or
fragrance and gold parfum et or
gong gong^{nom} gong gong
my gong gong ma gong gong
good^{nom} bien
your good ta bien
good^{adj} bon
God does good Dieu fait bon
good afternoon^{exc} bon après-midi
good afternoon après-midi bon
good evening^{exc} bonne soirée
good evening soir bon
good job^{exc} bon travail

good morning^{exc} bonjour
good morning matin bon
goodness^{nom} bonté
goodness and mercy bonté et miséricorde
goosebumps^{nom} la chair de poule
your goosebumps ta la chair de poule
gossip^{nom} potins
gossip is potins est
govern^{act} gouverner
govern Ghana gouvernez Ghana
governance^{nom} gouvernance
good governance gouvernance bon
government^{nom.-es plural} gouvernement
your government ta gouvernement
governor^{nom} gouverneur
she is the governor ell'est la gouverneur
grab^{act} saisir
grab his hand saisissez sa main

grace^nom grace
the grace of god la grace de dieu
graduate^nom diplômé
she is a graduate ell'est un diplômé
gramme^nom gramme
her gramme sa gramme
grandchild^nom petit-enfant
your grandchild ton petit-enfant
granddaughter^nom.-es plural petite fille
our granddaughter notre petite fille
grandfather^nom grand-père
my grandfather ma grand-père
grandma^nom grand-mère
my grandma ma grand-mère
grandson^nom petit fils
my grandson mon petit fils
grass^nom herbe
a cow chew grass un vache mâchez herbe
grasshopper^nom sauterelle
ant and grasshopper fourmi et sauterelle
gray^adj gris
gray hair cheveux gris
grease^nom graisse
grease graisse
great^adj grand
God is great Dieu est grand
great-grandchild^nom arrière petit-enfant
his great-grandchild son arrière petit-enfant
greed^nom avidité
gred and envy avidité et envie
greedy^adj glouton
greedy fool imbécile glouton
green^adj vert
the leaf is green la feuill'est vert
greenish^adj verdâtre
greenish house maison verdâtre
greet^act saluer
greet Ama saluez Ama
grief^nom douleur
grief is douleur est
grieve^act chagriner
my soul grieves ma âme chagrine
grind^act moudre
I grind je mouds
groin^nom aine
groin of a man aine de un homme
groundnut^nom arachide
corn and groundnut maïs et arachide

grove^nom bosquet
her grove sa bosquet
growth^nom.-es plural croissance
growth is good croissance est bon
guard^act garder
guard the house gardez la maison
guava^nom goyave
the guava is sweet la goyave est doux
guide^act guider
you guide tu guides
Guinea^nom Guinée
her Guinea sa Guinée
guinea-fowl^nom pintade
her guinea-fowl sa pintade
gun^nom pistolet
a soldier has a gun un soldat a un pistolet
gutter^nom caniveau
your gutter ta caniveau
guy personne mâle

habit^nom habitude
bad habit habitude mauvais
habitat^nom habitat
your habitat ta habitat
hair^nom cheveux
chest hair poitrine cheveux
half^nom moitié
one and half un et moitié
hall^nom salon
a big hall un salon grand
hallelujah^exc alléluia
sing hallelujah chantez hallelujah
hammer^nom marteau
her hammer sa marteau
hammock^nom hamac
your hammock ta hamac
hand^nom main
her hand sa main
handkerchief^nom mouchoir
my handkerchief ma mouchoir
hang^act pendre
hang it pendsez il
happen^act passer
she happens elle passe
happiness^nom bonheur
happiness has bonheur a
happy birthday^exc bon anniversaire
happy birthday Doris bon anniversaire Doris

happy new year^{exc} bonne année

happy new year bonne année

harass^{act} harceler

she harassed the dog ell'harcelait le chien

hard^{adj} difficile

the work is hard le travail est difficile

hard^{adv} difficilement

hardship^{nom} difficultés

great hardship difficultés grand

harmattan^{nom} Harmattan

harmattan brings dust Harmattan apporte poussière

hat^{nom} chapeau

my hat ma chapeau

hate^{act} haïr

you hate tu haïr

Hausa^{nom} Haoussa

I speak Hausa je dis Haoussa

have^{act} avoir

she has money ell'a argent

having^{pro} ayant

tea of sugar thé de sucre

hawk^{nom} faucon

a hawk and a chicken un faucon et un poulet

he^{pro} il

he eats the food il mange la nourriture

head^{nom} tête

your big head ta tête grand

headache^{nom} mal de tête

headache and fever mal de tête et fièvre

headgear^{nom} coiffures

your headgear ta coiffures

headscarf^{nom} foulard

my headscarf ma foulard

heal^{act} guérir

heal disease guérissez maladie

healing^{nom} guérison

your healing ta guérison

health^{nom} santé

food gives health nourriture donne santé

heap^{nom} tas

a heap of sand un tas de sable

hear^{act} entendre

she hear the whistle ell'entendsez la sifflet

heart^{nom} cœur

good heart cœur bon

heartburn^{nom} brûlures d'estomac

I have heartburn je avez brûlures d'estomac

heavy^{adj} lourd

the stone is heavy la pierre est lourd

hedgehog^{nom} hérisson

her hedgehog sa hérisson

heel^{nom} talon

toe and heel orteil et talon

heh^{exc} heh

sorry, heh sorry, heh

height^{nom} hauteur

height and width hauteur et largeur

helicopter^{nom} hélicoptère

her helicopter son hélicoptère

help^{act} aider

you help tu aides

heptagon^{nom} septagon

a heptagon has seven un septagon a sept

her^{pos} sa

her house sa maison

her^{pro} elle

show her montrer elle

here^{nom} ici

here and there ici et là

here^{adv} ici

click here cliquez ici

herpes^{nom} herpès

herpes is a disease herpès est un maladie

herring^{nom} hareng

a herring is a fish un hareng est un poisson

hers^{pro} la sienne

this thing is hers ce chose est la sienne

hexagon^{nom} hexagone

a hexagon has six un hexagone a six

hi^{exc} salut

hiccups^{nom} hoquet

my hiccups ma hoquet

hide^{act} cacher

to hide behind the door cacher derrière la porte

highway^{nom} autoroute

your highway ta autoroute

hill^{nom} colline

hill top colline top

him^{pro} lui

show him montrer lui

himself^{pro} lui-même

he respects himself il respect lui-même

hip^{nom} hanche
 your hip ta hanche
hiplife^{nom} hiplife
 hiplife is music hiplife est musique
hippopotamus^{nom} hippopotame
 a hippopotamus has a big belly un hippopotame
 a un estomac grand
his^{pos} sa
 his house sa maison
his^{pro} son
 this thing is his ce chose est son
history^{nom} histoire
 learn history apprendsez histoire
hit^{act} frapper
 he hits il frappe
hmph^{exc} hmph

hoe^{nom} houe
 hoe and cutlass houe et coutelas
hold^{act} tenir
 hold the bottle tenir la bouteille
hole^{nom} trou
 small hole trou petit
holy^{adj} saint
 this book is holy ce livre est saint
home^{nom} maison
 your home ta maison
homeless^{adj} sans abri
 a homeless person un personne sans abri
hometown^{nom} ville natale
 my hometown ma ville natale
honesty^{nom.y->ies plural} honnêteté
 honesty is good honnêteté est bon
honey^{nom} miel
 honey is sweet miel est doux
honour^{nom} honneur
 honour and love honneur et amour
hope^{nom} espoir
 I have hope je avez espoir
horn^{nom} corne
 horn music corne musique
horse^{nom} cheval
 white horse cheval blanc
hot^{adj} chaud
 the water is hot l'eau est chaud
hotel^{nom} hôtel
 she sleeps at a hotel

hour^{nom} heure
 your hour ta heure
house^{nom} maison
 the house la maison
housefly^{nom} mouche
 a housefly can
housekeeper^{nom.-es plural} gourvenante
 you need a housekeeper tu as besoin de une gourvenante
how^{adv} comment
 how comment
how are you^{exc} comment allez-vous
 how do you do are hello and bonjour et comment
 allez-vous
how much^{adj} combien
 it is how much il est combien
however^{cjn} cependant

huge^{adj} énorme
 a huge building un bâtiment énorme
human^{adj} humain
 we are human nous sommes humain
human^{nom} humain
 we are humans nous sommes humains
humankind^{nom} humanité
 humankind are good humanité sont bon
humble^{adj} humble
 humble person personne humble
humility^{nom} humilité
 you show humility tu montrez humilité
hundred^{adj} cent
 hundred cent
hunger^{nom} faim
 hunger and thirst faim et soif
hungry^{adj} affamé
 it is hungry il est affamé
husband^{nom} mari
 I love my husband j'aime ma mari
hydrogen^{nom} hydrogène
 hydrogen car hydrogène voiture
hyena^{nom} hyène
 my hyena ma hyène
I^{pro} je
 I eat the food je mange la nourriture
I am well^{exc} je vais bien
 I am well and thank you je vais bien et merci
if^{cjn} si

if ... then^{cjn} si ... alors
if A then B si A alors B
Igbo^{nom} Igbo
my Igbo ma Igbo
image^{nom} image
beautiful image image belle
immediately^{adv} immédiatement
cut coupez
immerse^{act} plonger
immerse him plongez lui
impertinence^{nom} impertinence
my impertinence ma impertinence
important^{adj} important
you are an important person tu es un personne important
in^{pre} dans
look in the pot regarder dans la pot
in front^{pre} devant
go in front allez dans avant
inactive^{adj} inactif
he is inactive il est inactif
increase^{act} augmenter
you increase tu augmentes
independence^{nom} indépendance
independence day indépendance jour
India^{nom} Inde
she loves India ell'aime Inde
Indian^{adj} indien
Indian Ocean Océan Indien
indigo^{adj} indigo
the cloth is indigo la chiffon est indigo
infertile^{adj} infertile
infertile land terre infertile
infinity^{nom} infini
infinity be not a number infini êt un numéro
information^{nom.y->ies plural} information
we have the information nous avons l'information

inheritance^{nom} héritage
claim your inheritance prétendsez ta héritage
injure^{act} blesser
we injure nous blessons
ink^{nom} encre
ink encre
inside^{adv} à l'intérieur
go inside allez inside
inside^{pre} à l'intérieur
inside the pot à l'intérieur la pot

insult^{act} insulter
the dog insults le chien insulte
insult^{nom} insulte
many insults insultes beaucoup
insults^{nom} insultes
unnecessary insults insultes inutile
integrate^{act} intégrer
we integrate nous intégrons
internet^{nom} Internet
internet link Internet lien
interrupt^{act} interrompre
interrupt him interrompsez him
intersection^{nom} jonction
her intersection sa jonction
investigation^{nom} enquête
they will do an investigation
Islam^{nom} Islam
your Islam ta Islam
Islamic^{adj} islamique
it is Islamic il est islamique
island^{nom} île
Seychelles island Seychelles île
issue^{nom} question
new issue question nouveau
it^{pro} il
it eats the food il mange la nourriture
it^{pro} ça

its^{pos} son
its house son maison
its^{pro} sa
its house son maison
ivory^{nom} ivoire
ivory necklace ivoire collier
jail^{nom} prison
go to jail allez à prison
jama^{nom} jama
we sing jama nous chantons jama
January^{nom} Janvier
January is a month Janvier est un mois
jar^{nom} pot
my jar ma pot
jaw^{nom} mâchoire
my jaw ma mâchoire
jester^{nom} bouffon
she is a jester ell'est un bouffon
Jesus^{nom} Jésus
her Jesus son Jésus

job^{nom} boulot
 I need a job je avez besoin de un boulot
join^{act} se raccorder
 words join mots se raccorder
joint^{nom} articulation
 my joint ma articulation
joke^{nom} blague
 her joke sa blague
jollof^{nom} jollof
 jollof is food jollof est nourriture
journalist^{nom} journaliste
 your journalist ta journaliste
journey^{nom} voyage
 a long journey un voyage longue
joy^{nom} joie
 joy and peace joie et paix
judge^{nom} juge
 my judge ma juge
judgement^{nom} jugement
 your judgement ta jugement
July^{nom} Juillet
 Friday. July 01, 1960 Vendredi. Juillet 01, 1960
jump^{act} sauter
 we jump nous sautons
June^{nom} Juin
 her June sa Juin
junk^{nom} jonque
 her junk sa jonque
just^{adj} juste
 it is just il est juste
just^{pre} juste
 just juste
just^{adv} juste
 just juste
justice^{nom} justice
 freedom and justice liberté et justice
k^{pho} k
 the sound of k la son de k
keep^{act} garder
 keep the change gardez la change
kenkey^{nom} kenkey
 kenkey and stew kenkey et ragoût
kente^{nom} kente
 kente cloth kente chiffon
Kenya^{nom} Kenya
 her Kenya sa Kenya
kerosene^{nom} kérosène
 bottle of kerosene bouteille de kérosène

key^{nom} clé
 your key ta clé
keyboard^{nom} clavier
 press "k" on the keyboard appuyer "k" sur la clavier

khakhi^{nom} khakhi
 khakhi shorts khakhi short
khebab^{nom} khebab
 her khebab sa khebab
kidney^{nom} rein
 a cat has a kidney un chat a un rein
kill^{act} tuer
 we kill nous tuons
kilometer^{nom} kilomètre
 her kilometer sa kilomètre
kind^{adj} gentil
 love is kind amour est gentil
kindle^{act} allumer
 kindle a fire allumez un feu
king^{nom} roi
 he is a king il est un roi
kingdom^{nom} royaume
 the kingdom of god la royaume de dieu
kiss^{act} baiser
 kiss baisez
kitchen^{nom} cuisine
 her kitchen sa cuisine
knee^{nom} genou
 your knee ta genou
knife^{nom} couteau
 sharpen a knife affilez un couteau
knot^{nom} nœud
 her knot sa nœud
know^{act} connaître
 I know je connaîtsez
knowledge^{nom} connaissance
 knowledge and wisdom connaissance et sagesse
kolanut^{nom} noix de cola
 your kolanut ta noix de cola
Kongo^{nom} Kikongo
 he records Kongo il écri Kikongo
koran^{nom} Coran
 the bible and the koran la bibl'et la Coran
laboratory^{nom} laboratoire
 a clinic laboratory un hôpital laboratoire
ladder^{nom} échelle
 long ladder échelle longue

lady^{nom} dame
lady Danso dame Danso
lake^{nom} lac
the lake has la lac a
lamb^{nom} agneau
lamb of god agneau de dieu
lamentation^{nom} lamentation
your lamentation ta lamentation
land^{nom} terre
buy land achetez terre
land^{act} atterrir
you land tu atterris
language^{nom} langue
meny languages langues beaucoups
lapse^{nom} faute
my lapse ma faute
laptop^{nom} portable
my laptop mon portable
last^{adj} dernier
he is last il est dernier
last^{adj}
last page page
lastborn^{nom} dernier-né
your lastborn ta dernier-né
late^{adv} en retard

later^{adv} plus tard

latrine^{nom} latrine
her latrine sa latrine
laugh^{act} rire
we laugh nous risons
laughter^{nom} rire

launder^{act} laver
I launder je lave
law^{nom} loi
the law says la loi di
lawyer^{nom} avocat
her lawyer sa avocat
lay^{act} mettre
she will lay on the ground
lazy^{adj} paresseux
the dog is lazy le chien est paresseux
lead^{act} conduire
lead us conduisez us
leader^{nom} chef
your leader ton chef

leaf^{nom} feuille
green leaf feuille vert
lean on^{act} s'appuyer sur
lean on me s'appuyer sur moi
learn^{act} apprendre
she learns ell'apprend
leave^{act} laisser
leave it laissez il
ledge^{nom} rebord
sleep the ledge dormez la rebord
left^{adj} gauche
we go left nous allons gauche
leg^{nom} jambe
swollen leg swollen jambe
lemon^{nom} citron
three lemons citrons troiss
lend^{act} prêter
lend me prêtez moi
length^{nom} longueur
height, width and length hauteur, largeur et longueur

leniency^{nom} clémence
your leniency ta clémence
lens^{nom} lentille
lens of a camera lentille de un appareil photographique

leopard^{nom} léopard
a leopard has a tail un léopard a un queue
leper^{nom} lépreux
my leper ma lépreux
leprosy^{nom} lèpre
leprosy is a disease lèpre est un maladie
lesson^{nom} leçon
learn the lesson apprendsez la leçon
let^{act} laisser
let laissez
let ... know^{act} informer
I let know je informe
letter^{nom} lettre
her letter sa lettre
liar^{nom} menteur
her liar sa menteur
liberty^{nom} liberté
your liberty ta liberté
library^{nom} bibliothèque
her library sa bibliothèque
lick^{act} lécher
we lick nous léchons

lid^nom couvercle
lid of a cup couvercle de un tasse
lie^nom mensonge
it is a lie il est un mensonge
lie^act mentir

life^nom vie
your life live well ta vie habites bien
lift^act soulever
I lift je souleve
light^nom lumière
light of the sky lumière de la ciel
lightning^nom foudre
lightning and thunder foudre et tonnerre
lightweight^adj léger
the book is lightweight le livre est léger
like^adv comme
it feels like fufu il sentit comme fufu
like^act aimer
I like eating
like^pre comme

lime^nom citron vert
lime juice citron vert juice
line^nom ligne
your line ta ligne
Lingala^nom Lingala
her Lingala sa Lingala
link^nom lien
internet link Internet lien
lion^nom lion
a lion has a tail un lion a un queue
lip^nom lèvres
my lip ma lèvres
lipbalm^nom baume à lèvres
your lipbalm ton baume à lèvres
lipstick beauté baume à lèvres

liquid^adj liquide
liquid water eau liquide
liquor^nom liqueur
pour a little liquor versez un liqueur petit
listen^act écouter
we listen nous écoutons
listener^nom auditeur
my listener ma auditeur
litigant^nom plaideur
she is a litigant ell'est un plaideur

litigation^nom litige
he likes litigation il aime litige
little^nom peu
my little ma peu
little^adj petit
pour a little liquor versez un liqueur petit
live^act habiter
you live tu habites
liver^nom foie
a dog has a liver un chien a un foie
living^adj vivant
living god dieu vivant
living-room^nom salle
his living-room sa salle
lizard^nom lézard
a lizard eats grass un lézard mange herbe
loan^nom prêt
I need a loan je avez besoin de un prêt
loan^act prêter
loan me prêtez moi
lobster^nom homard
I eat lobster je mangez homard
lodge^nom loge
my lodge ma loge
logo^nom logo
the logo of a business la logo de un affaires
long^adj longue
his beard is long sa barbe est longue
longevity^nom longévité
her longevity sa longévité
look^act regarder
look at the boy regardez à le garçon
loosen^act desserrer
we loosen nous desserrons
lose^act perdre
he lose his way il perdsez sa voie
louse^nom pou
my louse ma pou
love^act aimer
I love my wife j'aime ma femme
love^nom amour
peace and love paix et amour
lucky^adj chanceux
lucky girl fille chanceux
Luganda^nom Luganda
your Luganda ta Luganda
lump^nom morceau
a lump of gold un morceau de or

Luwo^{nom} Luwo
my Luwo ma Luwo
luxury^{nom} luxe
I see luxury je voyez luxe
machine^{nom} machine
new machine machine nouveau
madam^{nom} Madame
madam Mary Madame Mary
magazine^{nom} magazine
a new magazine un magazine nouveau
maggot^{nom} asticot
my maggot ma asticot
maid^{nom} femme de ménage
she is a maid ell'est un femme de ménage
maintain^{act} maintenir
he maintains a house il maintenit un maison
major^{adj} majeur
a major town un ville majeur
make^{act} faire
make food faites nourriture
Malagasy^{nom} Malgache
your Malagasy ta Malgache
malaria^{nom} paludisme
malaria is a disease paludisme est un maladie
male^{nom} homme
your male ta homme
man^{nom} homme
a tall man un homme grand
manage^{act} gérer
I manage je gére
manager^{nom} gestionnaire
a good manager un gestionnaire bon
mango^{nom} mangue
the mango has la mangue a
manner^{nom} manière
his manner is amusing sa manière est amusant
many^{adj} beaucoup
we have many nous avons beaucoup
map^{nom} carte
read the map lisez la carte
march^{act} défiler
the soldier will march la soldat défilera
March^{nom} Mars

market^{nom} marché
go to market allez à marché
marriage^{nom} mariage
good marriage mariage bon

marry^{act} marier
marry me mariez me
mass^{sci} masse
mass and energy masse et énergie
master^{nom} maître
master Kofi maître Kofi
masticate^{act} mastiquer
a cow masticates grass un vache mastique herbe
mat^{nom} tapis
her mat sa tapis
mathematics^{nom} mathématiques
she teaches mathematics ell'enseigne mathématiques
mattress^{nom} matelas
a new mattress un mateles nouveau
maximum^{adj} maximum
maximum amount montant maximum
May^{nom} Mai
my May ma Mai
maybe^{adv} peut-être
maybe peut-être
me^{pro} moi
me and you moi et tu
measure^{act} mesurer
measure two mesurez deux
meat^{nom} viande
goat meat chèvre viande
meet^{act} rencontrer
meet me rencontrez moi
meeting^{nom} réunion
cancel the meeting annulez la réunion
melon^{nom} melon
green melon melon vert
member^{nom,-es plural} membre
member of the team membre de l'équipe
memorization^{nom} mémorisation
some memorization is good quelques mémorisation est bon
memorize^{act} mémoriser
to memorize to mémorisez
memory^{nom} mémoire
computer memory ordinateur mémoire
mercy^{nom} miséricorde
goodness and mercy bonté et miséricorde
mere^{adj} simple
mere human humain simple
message^{nom} message
my message ma message

messengers^{nom} messagers
  the messengers have la messagers avez
metal^{nom} métal
  hat of metal chapeau de métal
meter^{nom} mètre
  my meter ma mètre
metre^{nom} mètre
  your metre ta mètre
mile^{nom} mile
  her mile sa mile
milk^{nom} lait
  milk and sugar lait et sucre
millet^{nom} mil
  millet porridge mil bouillie
million^{adj} million
  a million un million
mind^{nom} esprit
  her mind thinks an idea son esprit pense une idée

mine^{pro} mien
  the book is mine le livre est mien
minor^{adj} mineur
  a minor town un ville mineur
minute^{nom} minute
  your minute ta minute
mirror^{nom} miroir
  big mirror miroir grand
miser^{nom} avare
  he is a miser il est un avare
miserly^{adj} avare
  he is miserly il est avare
misfortune^{nom} malheur
  her misfortune sa malheur
miss^{act} manquer
  I miss home je manquez maison
missus^{nom} missus
  missus Clinton missus Clinton
mist^{nom} brume
  morning mist matin brume
mistress^{nom} maîtresse
  master and mistress maître et maîtresse
mix^{act} mélanger
  she mixs elle mélange
modern^{adj} moderne
  modern language langue moderne
moment^{nom} moment
  the moment is la moment est

Monday^{nom} Lundi
  her Monday sa Lundi
money^{nom} argent
  the money will help l'argent aidera
monitor^{nom} moniteur
  heart monitor cœur moniteur
monkey^{nom} singe
  a monkey eats banana un singe mange banane
month^{nom} mois
  she starts this month elle commence ce mois
moon^{nom} lune
  the moon and the sun la lune et le soleil
more^{adj} plus
  more food nourriture plus
more^{adv} plus
  to eat more manger plus
more than^{pre} plus que
  she eats more elle mange plus
morning^{nom} matin
  early morning matin de bonne heure
morsel^{nom} morceau
  two mouthfuls morceaux deux
mortar^{nom} mortier
  pestle and mortar pilon et mortier
mosque^{nom.-es plural} mosquée
  a new mosque une mosquée nouveau
mosquito^{nom} moustique
  a mosquito has un moustique a
mother^{nom} mère
  my mother ma mère
mountain^{nom} montagne
  mountain peak montagne peak
mouse^{nom} souris
  a big mouse un souris grand
mouse^{sci} souris
  computer mouse ordinateur souris
mouth^{nom} bouche
  my mouth ma bouche
mud^{nom} boue
  launder the mud lavez la boue
multiplication^{nom} multiplication
  your multiplication ta multiplication
murder^{nom} meurtre
  gossip and murder potins et meurtre
murderer^{nom} meurtrier
  he is a murderer il est un meurtrier
mushroom^{nom} champignon
  mushroom soup champignon soupe

music^nom musique
play music jeu musique
musician^nom musicien
her musician sa musicien
muslim^nom musulman
a Christian and a muslim un chrétien et un musulman
my^pos ma
my house ma maison
nail^nom ongle
nail and hammer ongl'et marteau
name^nom nom
my name ma nom
nation^nom nation
your nation ta nation
nausea^nom nausée
nausea and headache nausée et mal de tête
near^adv près
pull tirez
neck^nom cou
the tie hangs his neck la cravate pend son cou
necklace^nom collier
ivory necklace ivoire collier
need^act avoir besoin de
I need j'ai besoin de
needle^nom aiguille
string and needle chaîne et aiguille
neighbour^nom voisin
my neighbour ma voisin
nephew^nom neveu
my nephew ma neveu
nervous^adj nerveux
a nervous person un personne nerveux
network^nom réseau
the network la réseau
neutron^sci neutron

never^adv jamais
no, never non, jamais
new^adj nouveau
new family famille nouveau
news^nom nouvelles
news of the realm nouvelles du domaine
newspaper^nom journal
her newspaper sa journal
next^adj suivant
next page page suivant

nice^adj agréable
he is nice il est agréable
niece^nom nièce
your niece ta nièce
Niger^nom Niger
my Niger ma Niger
Nigeria^nom Nigeria
my Nigeria ma Nigeria
night^nom nuit
the night of Monday la nuit de Lundi
nightfall^nom tombée de la nuit
daybreak and nightfall aube et tombée de la nuit
nine^adj neuf
nine neuf
nine persons^nom neuf personnes
my nine persons ma neuf personnes
nineteen^adj dix-neuf
nineteen dix-neuf
nineteenth^adj dix-neuvième
the nineteenth dog le chien dix-neuvième
ninety^adj quatre-vingt dix
ninety quatre-vingt dix
no^exc non
I say "no" je dis "non"
Noah^nom Noé
my Noah mon Noé
noise^nom bruit
your noise ta bruit
nominate^act nommer
the dog nominates le chien nomme
nonagon^nom ennéagone
a nonagon has nine un ennéagone a neuf
noon^nom le midi
noon has le midi a
normal^adj normal
normal behaviour comportement normal
north^nom nord
go north allez nord
Norway^nom Norvège
your Norway ta Norvège
nose^nom nez
ear and nose oreill'et nez
not^adv pas
it is not a snake il est pas un serpent
nothing^nom rien
I have nothing je avez rien
noun^nom nom
the sentence has a noun la phrase a un nom

November^{nom} Novembre
my November ma Novembre
novice^{nom} novice
he is a novice il est un novice
now^{adv} maintenant
go now allez now
now^{cjn} maintenant

nucleus^{sci} noyau

number^{nom} numéro
number numéro
nurse^{nom} infirmière
she is a nurse ell'est un infirmière
nut^{nom} écrou
eat the nut manger l'écrou
oath^{nom} serment
great oath serment grand
obstacle^{nom} obstacle
her obstacle sa obstacle
ocean^{nom} océan
we see the ocean nous voyons l'océan
of^{pre} de
language of Africa langue de Afrique
office^{nom} bureau
the office of my mother la bureau de ma mère
often^{adv} souvent
she elle
oh^{exc} oh

oil^{nom} huile
the oil l'huile
okra^{nom} okro
okra soup okro soupe
old^{adj} vieux
old pan casserole vieux
old lady^{nom} vieille dame
my old lady ma vieille dame
old man^{nom} vieil homme
her old man sa vieil homme
on^{pre} sur
sleep the table dormez la table
one^{adj} un
it is one il est un
one person^{nom} une personne
your one person ta une personne
onion^{nom} oignon
a red onion une oignon rouge

only^{adj} seulement
only seulement
open^{act} ouvrir
I open the door je ouvrissez la porte
oppose^{act} opposer
I oppose the idea je oppose l'idée
oppress^{act} opprimer
you oppress tu opprimes
oppression^{nom} oppression
her oppression sa oppression
option^{nom} option
my option ma option
orange^{adj} orange
the light is orange la lumière est orange
orange^{nom} orange
her orange sa orange
Oromo^{nom} Oromo
her Oromo sa Oromo
ostentatious^{adj} ostentatoire
the dress is ostentatious la robe est ostentatoire
other^{adj} autre
an other time un temps autre
our^{pos} notre
our house notre maison
ours^{pro} les notres
this thing is ours ce chose est les notres
ourselves^{pro} nous-mêmes
we love ourselves nous aimons nous-mêmes
outdated^{adj} dépassé
outdated lorry camion dépassé
outdoors^{nom} à l'extérieur
go outdoors allez à l'extérieur
outside^{adv} dehors
stroll outside promenade extérieur
outside^{nom} extérieur
go outside allez extérieur
ovary^{nom} ovaire
her ovary sa ovaire
oware^{nom} oware
your oware ta oware
owe^{act} devoir
I owe you
owner^{nom} propriétaire
the owner of the car la propriétaire de la voiture
oxygen^{nom} oxygène
oxygen is in air oxygène est dans air
oyster^{nom} huître
I eat oyster je mangez huître

Pacific^{adj} pacifique
Pacific Ocean Océan Pacifique
pacify^{act} pacifier
pacify pacifier
pail^{nom} seau
pail and soap seau et savon
pain^{nom} douleur
the pain is where la douleur est où
paint^{act} peindre
he paints the wall il peind la mur
paint^{nom} peinture
white paint peinture blanc
palm^{nom} paume
a palm un paume
palmnut wool^{nom} laine palmnut
her palmnut wool sa laine palmnut
pan^{nom} casserole
old pan casserole vieux
pap^{nom} bouillie
eat the pap mangez la bouillie
papaya^{nom} papaye
papaya and banana papaye et banane
parable^{nom} parabole
her parable sa parabole
paralysis^{nom} paralysie
paraliesis is a disease paralysie est un maladie
parched^{adj} desséché
his skin is parched sa peau est desséché
parent^{nom.-es plural} parent
my parent mon parent
parents^{nom} parents
his parents sa parents
parliament^{nom} maison du parlement
your parliament ta maison du parlement
parrot^{nom} perroquet
her parrot sa perroquet
part^{nom} partie
my part ma partie
partner^{nom} partenaire
she is my partner ell'est ma partenaire
party^{nom} fête
your party ta fête
passion^{nom.-es plural} passion
she has passion ell'a passion
passport^{nom} passeport
your passport ton passeport
password^{nom} mot de passe
change password change mot de passe

paste^{act} coller
we paste nous collons
pastor^{nom} prêtre
my pastor ma prêtre
path^{nom} chemin
follow the path suitez la chemin
patience^{nom} patience
love and patience amour et patience
patient^{adj} patient
love is patient amour est patient
patient^{nom} patient
patriotism^{nom} patriotisme
he has patriotism il a patriotisme
pay^{act} payer
I pay je paye
peace^{nom} paix
the peace of God la paix de Dieu
peck^{act} picorer
she pecks elle picore
pedestrian^{nom} piéton
your pedestrian ta piéton
pedophile^{nom} pédophile
he is a pedophile il est un pédophile
peel^{act} peler
we peel nous pelons
peel off^{act} décoller
the dog peels off le chien décolle
pen^{nom} stylo
your pen ta stylo
pencil^{nom} crayon
take the pencil prendre le crayon
penguin^{nom.-es plural} manchot
a penguin is an animal un manchot est un animal
penis^{nom} pénis
my penis ma pénis
pentagon^{nom} pentagone
a pentagon has five un pentagone a cinq
people^{nom} gens
your people ta gens
pepper^{nom} poivre
the pepper la poivre
period^{nom} période
your period ta période
perjury^{nom} parjure
perjury of court parjure de tribunal

permanent[adj] permanent
the job is permanent le boulot est permanent
person[nom] personne
important person personne important
pesewa[nom] pesewa
one cedi makes a hundred pesewa cedi un fait un
pesewa cent
pestle[nom] pilon
pestle and mortar pilon et mortier
pet[nom] animal de compagnie
my pet mon animal de compagnie
philanderer[nom] coureur de jupons
her philanderer sa coureur de jupons
philanthropist[nom] philanthrope
she is a philanthropist ell'est un philanthrope
philosopher[nom] philosophe
she is a philosopher ell'est un philosophe
philosophy[nom] philosophie
my philosophy ma philosophie
phlegm[nom] flegme
wipe the phlegm essuyez la flegme
phone[act] téléphoner
you phone me tu téléphonez moi
phone[nom] téléphone
house phone maison téléphone
photograph[nom] photo
take a photograph prendsez un photo
physics[nom] physique
her physics sa physique
piano[nom] piano
my piano ma piano
pick up[act] ramasser
I pick up je ramasse
pierce[act] percer
pierce your ear percez ta oreille
pig[nom] porc
a pink pig un porc rose
pigeon[nom] pigeon
a pigeon is a bird un pigeon est un oiseau
pigfeet[nom] pigfeet
pigfeet soup pigfeet soupe
piglet[nom] porcelet
her piglet sa porcelet
pillar[nom] pilier

pimple[nom] bouton
I have a pimple je avez un bouton

pinch[act] pincer
you pinch tu pinces
pink[adj] rose
the pig is pink la porc est rose
pioneer[nom] pionnier
my pioneer ma pionnier
pipe[nom] tuyau
pipe water tuyau eau
pit[nom] fosse
dig a pit creusez un fosse
pitiful[adj] pitoyable
the child is pitiful l'enfant est pitoyable
pizza[nom] pizza
my pizza ma pizza
place[nom] place
your place ta place
plague[nom] fléau

plan[act] planifier
they plan elles planifient
planet[nom] planète
earth is a planet terre est une planète
plant[act] planter
she plants elle plante
plant[nom] plante
red plant plante rouge
plantain[nom] plantain
plantain and cassava plantain et manioc
plastic[adj] plastique
plastic cup tasse plastique
play[act] jouer
she plays elle joue
play[nom] jeu
my play ma jeu
pleasant[adj] agréable
a pleasant person un personne agréable
please[adv] s'il vous plaît
please and thank you s'il vous plaît et merci
pleasure[nom] plaisir
how do you do sr pleasure montrez ta plaisir
plentiful[adj] copieux
the food is plentiful la nourriture est copieux
plenty[adj] beaucoup
it is plenty il est beaucoup
pocket[nom] poche
her pocket sa poche
poem[nom.-es plural] poème
he records a poem il écri un poème

pointer^{nom} pointeur
use the pointer utilisez la pointeur
police^{nom} police
five police police cinq
politics^{nom} politique
you like politicss tu aimez politiques
poor^{adj} pauvre
a poor country un pays pauvre
porcupine^{nom} porc-épic
porcupine hole porc-épic trou
pork^{nom} porc
pork and beef porc et bœuf
porpoise^{nom} marsouin
your porpoise ta marsouin
porridge^{nom} bouillie
millet porridge mil bouillie
porter^{nom} portier
the porter carry a box la portier portez un boîte
position^{nom} position
a good position un position bon
possible^{adj}
evil is possible mal est
post office^{nom} bureau de poste
her post office sa bureau de poste
pot^{nom} pot
metal pot métal pot
pound^{act} frapper
I pound fufu je frappez fufu
pour^{act} verser
pour water versez eau
poverty^{nom} pauvreté
poverty or wealth pauvreté ou richesse
powder-keg^{nom} poudrière
your powder-keg ta poudrière
powerful^{adj} puissant
the engine is powerful le moteur est puissant
praise^{act} louer
you praise tu loues
praise^{nom} éloge
she deserves praise elle mérite éloge
pray^{act} prier
we pray nous prions
prayer^{nom} prière
prayer is good prière est bon
preacher^{nom} prédicateur
she is a preacher ell'est un prédicateur
preface^{nom} préface
book preface livre préface

pregnancy^{nom} grossesse
my pregnancy is easy ma grossesse est facile
pregnant^{adj} enceinte
a pregnant woman un femme enceinte
preparation^{nom} préparation
make preparation faites préparation
prepare^{act} préparer
the pastor will prepare la prêtre préparera
preservative^{nom} conservateur
her preservative sa conservateur
preserve^{act} préserver
I preserve je préserve
president^{nom} président
the president has la président a
press^{act} appuyer
you press tu appuyes
pretty^{adj} joli
the flower is pretty la fleur est joli
price^{nom} prix
what is the price la prix est que
pride^{nom} fierté
his pride sa fierté
print^{act} imprimer
we print nous imprimons
printer^{nom} imprimeur
book printer livre imprimeur
priority^{nom} priorité
what is your priority ta priorité est que
problem^{nom} problème
my problem ma problème
proclamation^{nom} proclamation
proclamation of the proclamation de la
procrastination^{nom} procrastination
procrastination is procrastination est
product^{nom} produit
make a product faire un produit
professor^{nom} enseignant
I am a professor je suis un enseignant
profit^{nom} profit
make profit faites profit
project^{nom} projet
my project ma projet
promise^{nom} promesse
your promise ta promesse
promise^{act} promettre
we promise nous promettsons
prop^{act} soutenir
prop the door soutenissez la porte

prophet^{nom} prophète
 powerful prophet prophète puissant
proprietor^{nom} propriétaire
 she is a proprietor ell'est un propriétaire
prosperity^{nom} prospérité
 peace and prosperity paix et prospérité
protect^{act} protéger
 protect us protégez us
protection^{nom} protection
 your protection ta protection
proton^{sci} proton
 the electric charge of a proton is +1 la charge électrique de un proton est +1
proverb^{nom} proverbe
 learn a proverb apprendre un proverbe
public^{nom} public
 my public ma public
pull^{act} tirer
 we pull nous tirons
pungently^{adv} mordant
 smell pungently odeur pungently
punish^{act} punir
 punish him punissez him
pure^{adj} pur
 pure gold or pur
purple^{adj} pourpre
 the flower is purple la fleur est pourpre
pursue^{act} poursuivre
 pursue him poursuitez him
push^{act} pousser
 I push je pousse
puzzle^{nom} puzzle
 your puzzle ta puzzle
python^{nom} python
 a python is a snake un python est un serpent
quake^{act} secouer
 we quake nous secouons
quality^{nom.y->ies plural} qualité
 the quality of the book la qualité du livre
quantity^{nom} quantité
 quantity of the food quantité de la nourriture
quarrel^{nom} querelle
 a big quarrel un querelle grand
queen^{nom} reine
 she is a queen ell'est un reine
question^{nom} question
 I have a question j'ai un question

quick^{adj}
 it is quick il est
quiet^{adj} calme
 they are quiet elles sont calme
rabbit^{nom} lapin
 a white rabbit un lapin blanc
race^{nom} course
 run a race courissez un course
rain^{nom} pluie
 the farmer wants rain l'agriculteur vouloit pluie
rainbow^{nom} arc-en-ciel
 I see a rainbow je voyez un arc-en-ciel
rainy^{adj} neigeux
 a rainy day un jour neigeux
raise^{act} augmenter
 raise your hand augmentez ta main
raisin^{nom} raisin
 eat the raisin mangez la raisin
ransom^{nom} rançon
 pay a ransom payez un rançon
rap^{nom} rap
 rap music rap musique
rat^{nom} rat
 a big rat un rat grand
razor^{nom} rasoir
 sharpen the razor affilez la rasoir
reach^{act} atteindre
 tomorrow, he will reach the house demain, il atteindra la maison
read^{act} lire
 read the book lire le livre
reading^{nom} lecture
 repeat the reading répétez la lecture
realm^{nom} domaine
 news of the realm nouvelles du domaine
rearguard^{nom} arrière-garde
 my rearguard ma arrière-garde
reason^{nom} raison
 my reason ma raison
rebel^{nom} rebelle

rebellion^{nom} la rébellion
 the rebellion has la la rébellion a
record^{act} écrire
 we record a letter nous écrisons un lettre
rectangle^{nom} rectangle
 a rectangle has four un rectangl'a quatre

red^{adj} rouge
red rouge
reflection^{nom} réflexion
his reflection sa réflexion
refuge^{nom} refuge
our refuge notre refuge
reject^{act} rejeter
I reject je rejete
rejoice^{act} réjouir
rejoice, I réjouissez, je
remain^{act.-es plural} rester
we remain nous restons
remainder^{nom} reste
the remainder of the food la reste de la nourriture

remember^{act} souvenir
me remember you moi souvenissez tu
remind^{act} rappeler
you remind tu rappeles
remove^{act} enlever
you remove tu enleves
repeat^{act} répéter
repeat the reading répétez la lecture
repent^{act} se repentir
she repents elle se repentir
repentance^{nom} repentance
love and repentance amour et repentance
replace^{act} remplacer
replace me remplacez moi
report^{nom} rapport
make a report faites un rapport
request^{act} demander
you request tu demandes
rescue^{act} sauver
she will rescue me elle sauvera moi
respect^{act} respect
I respect the child je respect l'enfant
respect^{nom} respect
love and respect amour et respect
responsible^{adj}
he is a responsible man il est un homme
restaurant^{nom} restaurant
a new restaurant un restaurant nouveau
resurrection^{nom} résurrection
the resurrection of Christ la résurrection de Christ

return^{act} retour
we return nous retour

reveal^{act} révéler
reveal the truth révélez la vérité
revelation^{nom} révélation
my revelation ma révélation
revival^{nom} renouveau
revival has renouveau a
revive^{act} relancer
revive yourself relancez yourself
rheumatism^{nom} rhumatisme
rheumatism is a disease rhumatisme est un maladie
rice^{nom} riz
rice and beans riz et haricots
rich^{adj} riche
a rich country un pays riche
riddle^{nom} énigme
my riddle ma énigme
right^{adj} droit
we go right nous allons droit
rights^{nom} droits
you have rights tu as droits
ringworm^{nom} teigne
he has ringworm il a teigne
ripen^{act} mûrir
I ripen je mûris
rival^{nom} rival
she is my rival ell'est ma rival
rivalry^{nom} rivalité
my rivalry ma rivalité
river^{nom} rivière
a river and the sea un rivière et la mer
road^{nom} rue
new road rue nouveau
roast^{act} rôtir
roast a little corn rôtissez un maïs petit
rock^{nom} rocher
a big rock un rocher grand
rocket^{nom.-es plural} fusée
we will build a big rocket nous construirons une fusée grand
room^{nom} chambre
her room sa chambre
root^{nom} racine
root of a tree racine de un arbre
rope^{nom} corde
a long rope un corde longue
rot^{act} pourrir
you rot tu pourris

row[nom] rangée
her row sa rangée
rubbish[nom] ordures
her rubbish sa ordures
rule[nom] règle
she follows the rule elle suiv la règle
rum[nom] rhum

rump[nom] croupe
look at his rump regardez à sa croupe
run[act] courir
we run nous courissons
sabotage[nom] sabotage
her sabotage sa sabotage
sack[nom] sac
sack of charcoal sac de charbon de bois
sad[adj] triste
a sad face un visage triste
salt[nom] sel
sugar and salt sucre et sel
salvation[nom] salut
your salvation ta salut
same[adj]
it is same il est
sand[nom] sable
beach sand plage sable
Saturday[nom] Samedi
my Saturday ma Samedi
saucepan[nom] casserole
cook in the saucepan cuisez dans la casserole
savant[nom] savant
my savant ma savant
save[act] enregistrer
save it enregistrez it
saw[nom] scie
her saw sa scie
say[act] dire
I say je disez
say goodbye[act] dire au revoir
you say goodbye tu dis au revoir
scar[nom] cicatrice
her cheek has a scar sa joue a un cicatrice
scarcity[nom] rareté
scarcity of water rareté de eau
scare[act] effrayer
we scare nous effrayons
scarlet[adj] écarlate
a scarlet dress un robe écarlate

scary[adj] effrayant
the film is scary la film est effrayant
scholarship[nom] bourse
I have a scholarship je avez un bourse
school[nom] école
your school ton école
scissors[nom] ciseaux
my scissors ma ciseaux
scrape[act] gratter
you scrape tu grattes
scripture[nom] Écriture
my scripture ma Écriture
search[act] rechercher
search his house recherchez sa maison
second[nom] seconde
her second sa seconde
secret[nom] secret
I have a secret je avez un secret
secret[adj]
his work is secret son travail est
sector[nom] secteur
her sector sa secteur
see[act] voir
you see tu vois
seed[nom] graine
three orange seed graine orange trois
seldomly[adv.foreign import] peu souvent
she comes seldomly here elle venit peu souvent ici

select[act] sélectionner
we select nous sélectionnons
selfishness[nom] égoïsme
selfishness is égoïsme est
sell[act] vendre
she sells elle vend
send[act] envoyer
send me envoyez me
sense[act] sentir
I sense je sentissez
sentence[nom] phrase
your sentence ta phrase
September[nom] Septembre
her September sa Septembre
servant[nom] serviteur
my servant ma serviteur
service[nom] service
your service is good ta service est bon

settle^{act} régler
settle there réglez là
seven^{adj} sept
seven sept
seven persons^{nom} sept personnes
your seven persons ta sept personnes
seventeen^{adj} dix-sept
it is seventeen il est dix-sept
seventy^{adj} soixante-dix
it is seventy il est soixante-dix
several^{adj} plusieurs
several plusieurs
sew^{act} coudre
sew cloth coudsez chiffon
sexy^{adj} sexy
a sexy man un homme sexy
shade^{nom} ombre
your shade ta ombre
shame^{nom} honte
shame and disgrace honte et disgrâce
shape^{nom} forme
the shape of the house la forme de la maison
share^{nom} part
your share ta part
share^{act} partager
you share tu partages
sharpen^{act} affiler
sharpen a knife affilez un couteau
she^{pro} elle
she eats the food elle mange la nourriture
sheabutter^{nom} beurre de karité
the fragrance of sheabutter la parfum de beurre de karité
sheep^{nom} mouton
the sheep sleeps
shell^{nom} coquille
shell of a crab coquille de un crabe
shield^{nom} bouclier
he is my shield il est ma bouclier
shine^{act} briller
she shines elle brille
ship^{nom} navire
a big ship un navire grand
shirt^{nom} chemise
my shirt ma chemise
shoe^{nom} chaussure
your shoe ta chaussure

Shona^{nom} Shona
her Shona sa Shona
shoot^{act} tirer
we shoot nous tirons
shop^{nom} boutique
my shop ma boutique
short^{adj} petit
this man is short ce homme est petit
shorts^{nom} short
khakhi shorts khakhi short
shoulder^{nom} épaule
her shoulder sa épaule
shout^{act} crier
I shout je crie
show^{act} montrer
we show nous montrons
shrimp^{nom} crevette
my shrimp ma crevette
shut^{act} fermer
shut the door fermez la porte
shy^{adj}
a shy woman un femme
sibling^{nom} enfant de mêmes parents
my sibling ma enfant de mêmes parents
sigh^{act} soupir
you sigh tu soupis
sighing^{nom} soupirs
your sighing ta soupirs
sign^{nom} signe
a sign of hope un signe de espoir
signify^{act} signifier
we signify nous signifions
silence^{nom} silence
your silence ta silence
silk^{nom} soie
white silk soie blanc
silver^{nom} argent
silver and gold argent et or
sin^{nom} péché
sin and forgiveness péché et pardon
sing^{act} chanter
we sing nous chantons
singleton^{nom} singleton

sink^{nom} évier
drain the sink vidangez l'évier
sink^{act} couler
we sink nous coulons

sir^{nom} Monsieur
her sir sa Monsieur
sister^{nom} sœur
his sister sa sœur
sit^{act} s'asseoir
sit here s'asseoir ici
six^{adj} six
six six
six persons^{nom} six personnes
my six persons ma six personnes
sixteen^{adj} seize
sixteen seize
sixteenth^{adj} seizième
the sixteenth house la maison seizième
sixty^{adj} soixante
sixty soixante
skill^{nom} compétence
your skill ta compétence
skin^{nom} peau
dry skin peau sec
skull^{nom} crâne
my skull ma crâne
sky^{nom} ciel
the sky and the sun la ciel et le soleil
slap^{act} gifler
slap him giflez him
slate^{nom} ardoise
wipe the slate essuyez l'ardoise
slave^{nom} esclave
my slave ma esclave
slavegirl^{nom} slavegirl
your slavegirl ta slavegirl
sleep^{act} dormir
you sleep tu dors
slim^{adj} mince
the man is slim l'homme est mince
slippers^{nom} pantoufle
your slippers ta pantoufle
slow^{adj} lent
the tortoise is slow la tortue est lent
slowly^{adv} lentement
a tortoise walks un tortue marche
small^{adj} petit
a small thing un chose petit
smaller^{adj} petit
smaller house maison petit
smell^{act} sentir
I smell je sentis

smell^{nom} odeur
I sense a smell je sentissez un odeur
smile^{act} sourire
we smile nous sourisons
smoke^{nom} fumée
belch smoke rotez fumée
smoothen^{act} lisser
she smoothens elle lisse
snail^{nom} escargot
I eat snails je mangez escargots
snake^{nom} serpent
a snake have not a leg un serpent avo un jambe
sneeze^{act} éternuer
we sneeze nous éternuons
snore^{act} ronfler
I snore I ronflez
snoring^{nom} ronflement
loud snoring ronflement bruyant
snow^{nom} neige
her snow sa neige
snowy^{adj} neigeux
today is snowy aujourd'hui est neigeux
snuff^{nom} tabac à priser
your snuff ta tabac à priser
so^{cjn} ainsi
why so? why so?
soap^{nom} savon
soap and water savon et eau
soccer^{nom} football
your soccer ta football
sock^{nom} chaussette
her sock sa chaussette
sofa^{nom} canapé
my sofa mon canapé
soft^{adj} doux
the bread is soft le pain est doux
soften^{act} adoucir
soften your voice adoucissez ta voix
soldier^{nom} soldat
the soldier and the police la soldat et la police
sole^{nom} semelle
my sole ma semelle
solid^{adj} solide
solid water eau solide
solution^{nom.-es plural} solution
we have a solution nous avons une solution
Somalia^{nom} Somalie
your Somalia ta Somalie

some^{pro} certains
some will come certains veniront
some^{det} quelques
some food quelques nourriture
somebody^{pro} quelqu'un
she loves somebody ell'aime quelqu'un
something^{pro} quelque chose
they want something elles vouloissent quelque chose

something^{nom} quelque chose
her something sa quelque chose
sometimes^{adv} parfois
we drink sometimes nous boisons parfois
somewhere^{pro} quelque part
we will go somewhere nous irons quelque part
son^{nom} fils
my son ma fils
song^{nom} chanson
play a song jouer un chanson
soon^{adv} bientôt
she is ell'est
soot^{nom} suie
black soot suie noir
sorcery^{nom} sorcellerie
practise sorcery practise sorcellerie
sore^{nom} plaie
her sore sa plaie
sorry^{exc} pardon
sorry, sorry pardon, pardon
soul^{nom} âme
my soul exults ma âme exulte
sound^{nom} son
loud sound son bruyant
soup^{nom} soupe
her soup sa soupe
south^{nom} sud
go south allez sud
sow^{act} semer
sow a tree semez un arbre
spade^{nom} pelle
my spade ma pelle
speak^{act} dire
she speaks elle di
spear^{nom} lance
one spear and one gun lance un et pistolet un
special^{adj} spécial
special day jour spécial

specific^{adj} spécifique
it is specific il est spécifique
spectacles^{nom} lunettes
he needs new spectacles il a besoin de lunettes nouveau
spectator^{nom} spectateur
your spectator ta spectateur
spider^{nom} araignée
her spider sa araignée
spine^{nom} colonne vertébrale
ear, nose and spine oreille, nez et colonne vertébrale

spinning top^{nom} toupie

spirit^{nom} esprit
he has a strong spirit il a un esprit fort
split^{act} séparer
split in two séparez dans deux
spokesperson^{nom} porte-parole
the spokesperson of a chief la porte-parole de un chef
sponge^{nom} éponge
my sponge ma éponge
sponsor^{nom} sponsor
your sponsor ta sponsor
spoon^{nom} cuillère
her spoon sa cuillère
sport^{nom} sport
she likes sports ell'aime sports
spouse^{nom} époux
my spouse mon époux
spread^{act} se répandre
spread it se répandre it
spread out^{act} étaler
he spreads out il étale
spy^{nom} espion
he is a spy il est un espion
spy^{act} espionner
we spy nous espionnons
squabbles^{nom} querelles
my squabbles ma querelles
squat^{act} s'accroupir
I squat je s'accroupis
squeeze^{act} presser
squeeze the orange pressez l'orange
squirrel^{nom} écureuil
a squirrel likes palm nut un écureuil aime paume écrou

stab^{act} poignarder
she stabs elle poignarde
stadium^{nom} stade
a new stadium un stade nouveau
staff^{nom} personnel
wooden staff wooden personnel
stair^{nom} escalier

stamp^{act} timbre
she stamps elle timb
stand^{act} se lever
you stand tu se lever
star^{nom} étoile
the sun is a star le soleil est une étoile
start^{act} commencer
we start nous commencons
state^{nom} état
my state ma état
statement^{nom.-es plural} déclaration
she records a statement ell'écri une déclaration
station^{nom} gare
train station train gare
steal^{act} voler
steal and destroy volez et détruisez
steer^{act} diriger
you steer tu diriges
step-child^{nom} beau-enfant
my step-child mon beau-enfant
stepfather^{nom.-es plural} beau-père
my stepfather likes the food mon beau-père aime la nourriture
stew^{nom} ragoût
make stew faites ragoût
stick^{nom} bâton
break the stick cassez la bâton
still^{adv} encore
still doing still doing
stinginess^{nom} avarice
her stinginess sa avarice
stir^{act} remuer
stir the porridge remuez la bouillie
stone^{nom} pierre
my stone ma pierre
stool^{nom} tabouret
sit the stool s'asseoissez la tabouret
storm^{nom} tempête
storm of thunder tempête de tonnerre

story^{nom} histoire
to tell a story raconter un histoire
straight^{adj} droit
the road is straight la rue est droit
stranger^{nom} étranger
your stranger ta étranger
stream^{nom} ruisseau
my stream ma ruisseau
street^{nom} rue
new street rue nouveau
strength^{nom} force
strength and authority force et puissance
string^{nom} chaîne
string and needle chaîne et aiguille
stroll^{nom} promenade
take a stroll prendsez un promenade
strong^{adj} fort
a strong woman un femme fort
student^{nom} étudiant
my student ma étudiant
studio^{nom.-es plural} studio
a music studio un musique studio
stumble^{act} trébucher
they stumble elles trébuchent
stump^{nom} souche
stump of a tree souche de un arbre
stupid^{adj}

submarine^{nom} sous-marin
a new submarine un sous-marin nouveau
subtract^{act} soustraire
subtract one soustraisez un
subtraction^{nom} soustraction
her subtraction sa soustraction
success^{nom} succès
success and happiness succès et bonheur
such as this^{exc} comme celle-ci
a person un personne
suck^{act} sucer
a baby sucks milk un bébé suce lait
suckle^{act} téter
suckle the breast tétez la poitrine
suddenly^{adv} tout à coup
it come il venissez
suffer^{act} souffrir
you suffer tu souffris
suffering^{nom} souffrance
my suffering ma souffrance

sugar^{nom} sucre
sugar and water sucre et eau
sugarcane^{nom} canne à sucre
your sugarcane ta canne à sucre
suit^{nom} costume
she wears a suit elle porte un costume
summit^{nom} sommet
mountain summit montagne sommet
sun^{nom} soleil
the sun and the moon le soleil et la lune
Sunday^{nom} Dimanche
her Sunday sa Dimanche
sunny^{adj} ensoleillé
a sunny day un jour ensoleillé
sunset^{nom} coucher du soleil

supply^{nom} offre
demand and supply demande et offre
surprise^{nom} surprise
great surprise surprise grand
surround^{act} entourer
you surround tu entoures
Swahili^{nom} Swahili
Swahili language Swahili langue
swallow^{act} avaler
she swallows ell'avale
swallow^{nom} hirondelle
a cat and a swallow un chat et un hirondelle
sweep^{act} balayer
she sweeps the floor elle balaye la sol
sweet^{adj} doux
the tea is sweet la thé est doux
sweet potato^{nom} patate douce
her sweet potato sa patate douce
swift^{nom.-es plural} Apodidae
the bird is a swift l'oiseau est un Apodidae
swim^{act} nager
I swim je nage
swing^{nom} balançoire
play a swing jouez un balançoire
switch off^{act} éteindre
you switch off tu éteinds
switch on^{act} allumer
you switch on tu allumes
symbol^{nom} symbole
symbol of authority symbole de puissance
syringe^{nom} seringue
my syringe ma seringue

table^{nom} table
chair and table chaise et table
tail^{nom} queue
a cat has a tail un chat a un queue
take^{act} prendre
we take nous prendsons
talk^{act} parler
you talk tu parles
tall^{adj} grand
the tree is tall l'arbre est grand
tap^{nom} robinet
open the tap ouvrissez la robinet
tarantula^{nom} tarentule
a large tarantula un tarentule grand
taste^{act} goût
taste the food goût la nourriture
tax^{nom} taxe
we pay the tax nous payons la taxe
taxi^{nom} taxi
my taxi ma taxi
tea^{nom} thé
the tea is sweet la thé est doux
teach^{act} enseigner
she teaches ell'enseigne
team^{nom} équipe
my team ma équipe
tear^{act} déchirer
tear déchirez
tear^{nom} larme
her tear sa larme
tease^{act} taquiner
tease him taquinez him
technical^{adj} technique
technical work travail technique
television^{nom} télévision
my television ma télévision
tell^{act} raconter
you tell tu racontes
temple^{nom.-es plural} temple
a new temple un temple nouveau
ten^{adj} dix
ten dix
termite^{nom} termites
her termite sa termites
test^{act} tester
the dog tests le chien teste
testament^{nom} testament
new testament testament nouveau

testicle^{nom} testicule
your testicle ta testicule
testimony^{nom} témoignage
what is your testimony ta témoignage est que
than^{cjn} que
he is tall il est grand
thank^{act} remercier
we thank nous remercions
thank you^{exc} merci
thank you, thank you merci, merci
thanks^{exc} merci
thanks Mandela merci Mandela
that^{pro} cette
that is yours cette est le tiens
that^{det} ce
that dog ce chien
that^{cjn} que
a child that walks un enfant que marche
that escalated quickly^{exc} qui sont intensifiés rapidement
my friend, that escalated quickly ma ami, qui sont
intensifiés rapidement
that person ce personne

that thing ce chose

the^{det} la
the man, the woman and the child l'homme, la
femme et l'enfant
the thing la chose

their^{pos} leur
their house leur maison
them^{pro} leur
show them montrez leur
themselves^{pro} eux-mêmes
they love themselves elles aiment eux-mêmes
then^{adv} puis
then puis
there^{nom} là
here and there ici et là
there^{adv} y
she will go there ell'ira y
these^{pro} ces
they see these elles voient ces
these^{det} ces
these books ces books

they^{pro} elles
they eat the food elles mangent la nourriture
thief^{nom} voleur
her thief sa voleur
thigh^{nom} cuisse
chicken thigh poulet cuisse
thin^{adj} mince
the girl is thin la fill'est mince
thing^{nom} chose
one thing chose un
things^{nom} des choses
your things tes des choses
think^{act} penser
I think every day je pense jour chaque
thirst^{nom} soif
I feel thirst je sentissez soif
thirsty^{adj} desséché
it is thirsty il est desséché
thirteen^{adj} treize
thirteen treize
thirteenth^{adj} treizième
the thirteenth day la jour treizième
thirty^{adj} trente
thirty trente
this^{pro} cet
this is yours cet est le tiens
this^{det} ce
lend me prêtez moi
though^{cjn} bien que

thought^{nom} pensées
her thought sa pensées
thousand^{adj} mille
thousand mille
thousands^{adj} milliers
it is thousands il est milliers
threat^{nom} menace

three^{adj} trois
three trois
three persons^{nom} trois personnes
her three persons sa trois personnes
throat^{nom} gorge
her throat sa gorge
throne^{nom} trône
her throne sa trône
throw^{act} jeter
she throws elle jete

throw away^{act} jeter
I throw away je jete
thumb^{nom} pouce
use your thumb utilisez ta pouce
thunder^{nom} tonnerre
storm of thunder tempête de tonnerre
Thursday^{nom} Jeudi
your Thursday ta Jeudi
ticket^{nom} billet
look at my ticket regardez à ma billet
tie^{act} attacher
we tie nous attachons
tie^{nom} cravate
the tie hangs his neck la cravate pend son cou
tie-and-dye^{nom} tie-and-dye
your tie-and-dye ta tie-and-dye
tiger^{nom} tigre
a large tiger un tigre grand
tigernut^{nom} souchet
her tigernut sa souchet
tightly^{adv} fermement
hold it tenissez il
time^{nom} temps
the time is la temps est
times^{nom} fois
ten times fois dix
tithe^{nom} dîme
pay your tithe payez ta dîme
title^{nom} titre
the title of a book la titre de un livre
to^{pre} à
from here to there de ici à là
tobacco^{nom} tabac
smoke tobacco fumée tabac
today^{adv} aujourd'hui
she arrives today ell'arrive aujourd'hui
toddler^{nom} bambin
toddler, where bambin, où
toe^{nom} orteil
toe and heel orteil et talon
toffee^{nom} caramel
lick a toffee léchez un caramel
together^{adv} ensemble

Togo^{nom} Togo
my Togo ma Togo
toilet^{nom} toilettes
go to the toilet allez à la toilettes

toilet roll^{nom} rouleau de papier toilette
one toilet roll rouleau de papier toilette un
tomato^{nom} tomate
your tomato ta tomate
tongue^{nom} langue
dog's tongue dog's langue
too^{adv} aussi
too slowly aussi lentement
too much^{adv} trop
he insult il insultez
tool^{nom} outil
her tool son outil
tooth^{nom} dent
white tooth dent blanc
toothbrush^{nom} brosse à dents
toothbrush and toothpaste brosse à dents et dentifrice
toothpaste^{nom} dentifrice
toothbrush and toothpaste brosse à dents et dentifrice
tortoise^{nom} tortue
a tortoise walks un tortue marche
total^{adj} total
the total amount le montant total
totally^{adv} totalement
it is il est
touch^{act} toucher
she touches elle touche
towel^{nom} serviette
wet towel serviette mouillé
town^{nom} ville

trade^{nom} commerce
a good trade un commerce bon
trade^{act} troquer
I trade je troque
trader^{nom} commerçant
I am a trader je suis un commerçant
tradition^{nom} tradition
your tradition ta tradition
traffic^{nom} circulation
traffic light circulation lumière
train^{nom} train
a new train un train nouveau
traitor^{nom} traître
your traitor ta traître
translate^{act} traduire
to translate English to Akan traduire Anglais à

Akan

transportation^{nom} transport
she has transportation ell'a transport
travel^{act} voyager
we travel nous voyageons
traveller^{nom} voyageur
my traveller ma voyageur
tray^{nom} plateau
your tray ta plateau
treasure^{nom} trésor
great treasure trésor grand
tremble^{act} trembler
you tremble tu trembles
trend^{nom} tendance
a good trend un tendance bon
triangle^{nom} triangle
a triangle has three un triangl'a trois
tribute^{nom.-es plural} hommage
they give a tribute elles donnes un hommage
trick^{nom} ruse

trillion^{adj} trillion
one trillion un trillion
trinity^{nom} trinité
holy trinity trinité saint
trip^{nom} voyage
trip of India voyage de Inde
triplets^{nom} triplés
my triplets ma triplés
trouble^{nom} difficulté
trouble and pain difficulté et douleur
true^{adj} vrai
the story is true l'histoire est vrai
truly^{adv} vraiment
truly vraiment
trumpet^{nom} trompette
her trumpet sa trompette
trust^{act} faire confiance
I trust je fais confiance
trust^{nom} confiance
my trust ma confiance
truth^{nom} vérité
she speak the truth elle disez la vérité
try^{act} essayer
try again essayez again
Tuesday^{nom} Mardi
my Tuesday ma Mardi

tumbler^{nom} verre
one tumbler of water verre un de eau
turbulent^{adj} turbulent
a turbulent world un monde turbulent
turkey^{nom} dinde
the meat of a turkey la viande de un dinde
turn off^{act} éteindre
you turn off tu éteins
tweet^{act} tweeter
a bird tweets un oiseau tweete
twelfth^{adj} douzième
the twelfth night la nuit douzième
twelve^{adj} douze
it is twelve il est douze
twentieth^{adj} vingtième
the twentieth book le livre vingtième
twenty^{adj} vingt
twenty vingt
twin^{nom} jumeau
she is a twin ell'est un jumeau
two^{adj} deux
it is two il est deux
two persons^{nom} deux personnes
my two persons ma deux personnes
type^{act} taper
I type je tapez
ugly^{adj} laid
it is ugly il est laid
ukelele^{nom} ukulélé
her ukelele sa ukulélé
umbrella^{nom} parapluie
sit under the umbrella s'asseoir en dessous de la parapluie
unappreciativeness^{nom} unappreciativeness
her unappreciativeness sa unappreciativeness
uncle^{nom} oncle
our uncle notre oncle
under^{adv} en dessous de
sit under the tree s'asseoir en dessous de l'arbre
understand^{act} comprendre
you understand tu comprends
unfamiliar^{adj} inconnu
the animal is unfamiliar l'animal est inconnu
ungrateful^{adj} ingrat
somebody is ungrateful quelqu'un est ingrat
union^{nom} union
African union African union

unit^{nom} unité
 your unit ta unité
unite^{act} unir
 we unite nous unissons
unity^{nom} unité
 unity and peace unité et paix
university^{nom} université
 your university ta université
unnecessary^{adj} inutile
 unnecessary insults insultes inutile
until^{pre} jusqu'à
 until jusqu'à
up^{adv} en haut
 look up regardez up
urinate^{act} uriner
 you urinate tu urines
urine^{nom} urine
 the urine l'urine
Ururimi^{nom} Ururimi
 my Ururimi ma Ururimi
us^{pro} nous
 show us montrez nous
use^{act} utiliser
 I use je utilise
user^{nom} utilisateur
 my user ma utilisateur
vaccinate^{act} vacciner
 she vaccinates elle vaccine
vagina^{nom} vagin
 your vagina ta vagin
valiant^{adj} vaillant
 it is valiant il est vaillant
valley^{nom} vallée
 your valley ta vallée
value^{nom} valeur
 I understand the value je comprends la valeur
vase^{nom} vase
 clay vase argile vase
vegetable oil^{nom} huile végétale
 your vegetable oil ta huile végétale
vehicle^{nom} véhicule
 a new vehicle un véhicule nouveau
vein^{nom} veine
 his vein sa veine
venom^{nom} venin
 venom of a snake venin de un serpent
verandah^{nom} véranda
 your verandah ta véranda

verb^{nom} verbe
 the sentence has a verb la phrase a un verbe
verse^{nom} verset
 her verse sa verset
version^{nom} version
 your version ta version
very^{adv} très
 you have tu avez
very desirable^{adj} très souhaitable
 it is very desirable il est très souhaitable
vibrate^{act} vibrer
 you vibrate tu vibres
vice^{nom} vice
 your vice ta vice
victory^{nom} victoire
 your victory ta victoire
video^{nom} vidéo
 watch the video regarder la vidéo
village^{nom} village
 I will visit the village je visiterai la village
violet^{adj} violet
 the paper is violet la journal est violet
virtue^{nom} la vertu
 your virtue ta la vertu
visit^{act} visiter
 I visit je visite
vitality^{nom} vitalité
 her vitality sa vitalité
vodka^{nom} vodka

voice^{nom} voix
 soften your voice adoucissez ta voix
volume^{nom} volume
 your volume ta volume
vomit^{nom} vomi
 clean the vomit nettoyer la vomi
vote^{act} voter
 you vote tu votes
voting^{nom} vote
 her voting sa vote
vulture^{nom} vautour
 your vulture ton vautour
wailing^{nom} lamentation
 her wailing sa lamentation
waist^{nom} taille
 your waist ta taille
wait^{act} attendre
 we wait nous attendsons

waiter^{nom} garçon
he is a waiter il est un garçon
wake^{act} reveiller
I wake je reveille
walk^{act} marcher
to walk slowly marcher lentement
wall^{nom} mur
sit the wall s'asseoissez la mur
want^{act} vouloir
I want the book je voulois le livre
war^{nom} guerre
your war ta guerre
warhorn^{nom} corne de guerre
my warhorn ma corne de guerre
warn^{act} avertir
warn someone avertissez someone
warning^{nom} avertissement
listen to the warning écoutez à l'avertissement
warrior^{nom} guerrier
warrior of antiquity guerrier de antiquité
warriors^{nom} guerriers

wasp^{nom} guêpe
her wasp sa guêpe
waste^{nom} déchets
her waste sa déchets
wasted^{adj} gaspillé
wasted food nourriture gaspillé
watch^{act} regarder
we watch nous regardons
water^{nom} eau
you drink the water tu bois l'eau
watermelon^{nom} pastèque
eat the watermelon mangez la pastèque
wave^{nom} vague

way^{nom} voie
the way la voie
we^{pro} nous
we eat the food nous mangeons la nourriture
weak^{adj} faible
I am weak je suis faible
weakness^{nom} faiblesse
in her weakness dans sa faiblesse
wealth^{nom} richesse
wealth or poverty richesse ou pauvreté
weapon^{nom} arme
your weapon ta arme

wear^{act} porter
wear clothes portez vêtements
weaverbird^{nom} tisserin
my weaverbird ma tisserin
web^{nom} toile
the web of a spider la toile de un araignée
website^{nom} site Web
your website ta site Web
wed^{act} se marier
she weds elle se marier
wedding^{nom} mariage
your wedding ta mariage
Wednesday^{nom} Mercredi
my Wednesday ma Mercredi
week^{nom} semaine
this week ce semaine
weigh^{act} peser
weigh your child pesez ta enfant
weight^{nom} poids
a heavy weight un poids lourd
welcome^{exc} bienvenue
welcome, welcome bienvenue, bienvenue
well^{adv} bien
do it faites il
well^{adj} bien
it is well il est bien
well^{nom} puits
her well sa puits
well done^{exc} bien fait
well done Sah bien fait Sah
west^{nom} ouest
go west allez ouest
wet^{adj} mouillé
wet blanket couverture mouillé
whale^{nom} baleine
a large whale un baleine grand
what^{pro} que
what is love amour est que
wheat^{nom} blé
my wheat ma blé
wheel^{nom} roue
your wheel ta roue
when^{cjn} quand
he come il venissez
where^{adv} où
where où
which^{det} quel
which child? quel child?

while^{cjn} tandis que

whine^{act} se plaindre
I whine je se plaindre
whip^{nom} fouet
horse whip cheval fouet
whistle^{nom} sifflet
blow the whistle souffler la sifflet
white^{adj} blanc
white house maison blanc
who^{pro} qui
who is he il est qui
whoa^{exc} holà

whole^{adj} entier
who is the moneyle l'argent est entier
why^{adv} pourquoi
why so? why so?
wicked^{adj} méchant
the animal is wicked l'animal est méchant
wickedness^{nom} méchanceté
your stinginess and your wickedness ta avarice et ta méchanceté
wide^{adj} large
wide road rue large
widow^{nom} veuve
she is a widow ell'est un veuve
widowed^{adj}
widowed man homme
widower^{nom} veuf
he is a widower il est un veuf
widowhood^{nom} veuvage
a short widowhood un veuvage petit
width^{nom} largeur
height and width hauteur et largeur
wife^{nom} femme
my wife and my child ma femme et ma enfant
wild^{adj} sauvage
wild animal animal sauvage
will^{nom} volonté
God's will God's volonté
win^{act} gagner
you win tu gagnes
wind^{nom} vent
the wind is la vent est
window^{nom} fenêtre
open the window ouvrir la fenêtre

windy^{adj} venteux
a windy day un jour venteux
wine^{nom} du vin
we drink wine nous boisons du vin
wing^{nom} aile
a bird has two wings un oiseau a ailes deux
wipe^{act} essuyer
she wipes ell'essuye
wisdom^{nom} sagesse
strength and wisdom force et sagesse
wise^{adj}
a wise girl une fille
wish^{act} souhaiter
she wishs elle souhaite
witch^{nom} sorcière
she is a witch ell'est un sorcière
witchcraft^{nom} sorcellerie
practise witchcraft practise sorcellerie
withdraw^{act} rétirer
he withdraws il rétire
witness^{nom} témoin
my witness ma témoin
wizard^{nom} sorcier
he is a wizard il est un sorcier
wolf^{nom} loup
my wolf ma loup
Wolof^{nom} Wolof
your Wolof ta Wolof
woman^{nom} femme
a pretty woman un femme joli
womb^{nom} utérus
the womb of a woman l'utérus de un femme
wonder^{nom} émerveillement
wonder and love émerveillement et amour
word^{nom} mot
your word ta mot
work^{act} travailler
we work nous travaillons
work^{nom} travail
the work is good le travail est bon
working^{nom} travail
working is travail est
workshop^{nom.-es plural} atelier
we have a workshop nous avons un atelier
world^{nom} monde
your world ton monde
worm^{nom} ver
worm, where ver, où

worry^{nom} souci
your worry ta souci
worship^{act} adorer
I worship je adore
wow^{exc} sensationnel

wrist^{nom} poignet
hold her wrist tenissez sa poignet
xylophone^{nom} xylophone
my xylophone mon xylophone
y^{pho.-es plural} y
y y
yam^{nom} igname
cook the yam cuisez l'igname
yard^{nom} cour
big yard cour grand
yawn^{act} bâiller
we yawn nous bâillons
yaws^{nom} pian
yaws is a disease pian est un maladie
ye^{pro} toi
me and ye moi et toi
year^{nom} année
a new year has un année nouveau a
yearly^{adj} annuel
it is yearly il est annuel
yell^{act} crier
you yell tu cries
yellow^{adj} jaune
the flag is yellow le drapeau est jaune
yes^{exc} oui
I say yes je dis oui
yet^{cjn} pourtant
the book is big le livre est grand
Yoruba^{nom} Yoruba
her Yoruba sa Yoruba
you^{pro} tu
you eat the food tu manges la nourriture
you^{pro} toi
I love you j'aimez toi
you^{pro} vous
you eat the food vous mangez la nourriture
you^{pro} vous
we greet you nous saluons vous
young^{adj} jeune
young person personne jeune
young boy^{nom} jeune garçon
her young boy sa jeune garçon

young man^{nom} jeun homme
my young man ma jeun homme
your^{pos} ta
your house ta maison
your^{pos} votre
you and you, your house tu et tu, votre maison
yours^{pro} le tiens
the book is yours le livre est le tiens
yourself^{pro} toi même
you love yourself tu aimes toi même
youth^{nom} jeunesse
my youth ma jeunesse
ytterbium^{sci} ytterbium
ytterbium is a ytterbium ytterbium est un ytterbium
Zambia^{nom} Zambie
my Zambia mon Zambie
Zambian^{adj}
the coffee is Zambian le café est
zebra^{nom} zèbre
her zebra sa zèbre
zero^{adj} zéro
zero and one zéro et un
Zulu^{nom} Zoulou
your Zulu ta Zoulou

French kasahorow

fr.kasahorow.org/app/l

- Modern French Verbs: Master the basic tenses of French

KWID: A-10000-FR-EN-2020-03-24

https://www.kasahorow.org/booktalk - Merci! Thank you!

Printed in Great Britain
by Amazon